PRAY FOR ONE

Bo Chancey

Pray for One
Published by 41Press

5 7 9 11 12 10 8 6 4

For information or bulk sales:

41PRESS
Attn: Publishing Team
7200 Queens Place
Amarillo, TX 79109

publisher@41press.com

ISBN: 978-0-9968757-2-1

Contents

GIVE ME ONE

chapter one

GIVE ME ONE

I begin with confession.

Confession generally makes everyone uncomfortable, so it is probably not the most strategic way to start a book. I guess that I am okay with this being a bit on the weird side. If you are like me, you have most likely tried normal and found it to be lacking in the satisfaction department.

So let us throw convention to the side and allow the awkwardness to ensue.

I confess that I believe in what Praying for One is all about to an extreme level. I am living out the methodology side of Praying for One. It is ingrained in my DNA. I am immersed in the results. I am a passionate believer in the transformational power of this simple prayer.

9

I confess that my zeal provides an edge to my words that may cut deeper than intended. I have no desire to wound needlessly, and I have no axe to grind, but my personal failures in following Jesus drive me to share the blessed hope of fruitful living with ever-increasing fervor.

I confess that I have wasted much of my life in vain attempts to make Christianity into something it cannot be. I have stumbled and bumbled through one self-generated mess after another. I have jumped on spiritual bandwagons, followed the hottest trends, and allowed Jesus to become little more than a pop-culture icon in my life. I tried to make Christianity about me instead of about Jesus. My primary motivation was for Jesus to serve me and make my life better instead of me serving Him to expand His Kingdom.

I confess that I have dabbled in many forms of legalism. Okay...that is not true. I have not just dabbled; I have been a full-on legalism addict. I have turned from grace to all kinds of rules and regulations. I know the foolishness of it, but my desire to compete and be better than other Christians was insatiable. I have slandered and demeaned other servants of Jesus because I felt inferior to them and I was jealous of their success.

I confess to feeling great frustration regarding my failures. I am saddened by the ways I have degraded the gospel of Jesus. I grieve over lost time and actions that were detrimental to others. I cannot stand the thought that others might have been following me when I was not in step with Christ. What manner of false doctrine might I have imparted to them?

I confess my tendency to project my flaws onto others. Any perceived finger pointing found within this book will include me at the front of the line. My intent is not to chastise but to encourage and inspire. I have found something great, and I want everyone to experience it.

I confess that I am afraid of what you will think of me. I want you to like me. I want you to like my book. I want you to think things like, "Wow, that Bo Chancey is one sharp cookie!" I don't even know what that means, but I want you to think it.

I confess the truth. I have found purpose beyond self. I have found meaning beyond mere religious expressions. I have found a practical way to connect to God, to others, and to the mission of Jesus.

Praying for One is awesome. I am in awe of how something so simple provides a path for deep growth and eternal fruit. The accessibility of this call to action removes discipleship barriers. Anyone can pray for One. There are no prerequisites. This prayer is a wonderful next step for anyone desiring to live the life for which we were all created.

Pray for One is not an evangelistic program or a trendy church-growth strategy. Pray for One is about becoming like Jesus and thus doing what He would do. Pray for One is discipleship in three words.

What was Jesus like? What motivated Him?

We see His heart very clearly when Jesus taught about a shepherd and his sheep. You see, Jesus is consumed with the One. What does He say? If a shepherd has 100 sheep and One of them wanders away, he will leave the 99 to look for the One. Jesus is that kind of shepherd, and He is passionately fixated on finding the One. If we are true followers of Jesus, then we too must become passionately consumed with His mission of finding the One.

The premise is simple, and it is imperative that we refrain from complicating it.

Just ask God to give you One person to share His love with. Pray that He would place someone, anyone, in your path to share the gospel with. As often as you pray, pray for One. Allow your primary prayers to move beyond prayers for self into prayers for One. Seek first His Kingdom and His righteousness. Instead of just praying for promotions, protection, and provision, plead first for One.

Bombard the throne with passionate prayers for One. Drive your God crazy with the zealous request for One. Approach the throne of grace with extreme confidence that you are requesting the expressed will of Christ as you pray for One.

What occurs when we pray for One is that our entire outlook on life changes. Instead of viewing people as nuisances, we see them as the One. People are no longer our competition or our enemies; they are objects of grace waiting to be found.

This is repentance at its finest. Repent is a wonderful word that means much more than just not sinning. Repent means to adopt a new worldview.

Praying for One will produce a new worldview as you see everything through the lens of Jesus and His mission to seek and save the lost. Scripture instructs us to offer our bodies as living sacrifices to the Lord and to be transformed by the renewing of our minds. When we do this we will know God's good, pleasing, and perfect will. Not only will we know it, we will want it too!

Praying for One will change your foundational purpose for living. Life will suddenly spring to life through the sincerity of this simple prayer. When you want what Jesus wants, life finally makes sense, and the joy of spiritual reproduction consumes you.

As our hearts change, we find that we are not too busy to speak to a neighbor or stay late with a coworker. We find that our heads are up and that we make eye contact with people because we never know who the One will be.

No day is wasted, because we arise in the morning with a true sense of mission and purpose. The first words on our lips are, "Give me One." The gospel becomes each day's destination.

Praying for One puts us into position to be fully used by God. This stuff is addictive. You get that first One and you can't stop. You have to have another and another and another. Kingdom growth becomes exponential. One becomes two, two becomes four, four becomes eight, eight becomes sixteen, and so on, as each of your Ones begins to pray for One too.

Why not start right now?

Let's pray.

"Give me One."

A challenge to try

ONCE YOU NAME IT...YOU ARE RESPONSIBLE FOR IT

chapter two

ONCE YOU NAME IT...YOU ARE RESPONSIBLE FOR IT

Praying for One begins with a rather general prayer asking God to give you One person to share His love with. The One could be anyone. This type of praying makes you evangelistically available at all times. You begin to look at everyone differently because they might be the answer to your prayer.

People that you might have otherwise ignored will suddenly have your undivided attention. You will listen for cues and conversational openings that enable you to thoughtfully share the love of Jesus. People are dying to hear about Jesus. As you pray for One, you will be amazed by how open people are to the story of Christ and His love.

Sometimes when praying for One, God will lay a specific name on your heart. Chances are that there is a family member, friend, neighbor, co-worker, etc., in your life who does not yet know Jesus. As you pray for One, you will probably end up praying for someone by name. When a specific name is on your heart, there is a responsibility to share God's love with them.

Praying daily for that person by name will cause you to look at them differently. They will become your One. You will not give up on them. You will not stop praying for them. You will take active steps to repeatedly share Jesus with them. You will feel responsible because you have a divine mission.

One morning, I was in our kitchen serving our three children breakfast. At the time, our oldest daughter Alizah was in the fifth grade, our son Ace was in the first grade, and our youngest daughter Ensley was still a year away from starting kindergarten.

The school year had just begun, and I was quizzing Alizah and Ace about how things were going. I was doing a little rapid fire Q and A with them about their teachers, classmates, subject matter, lunches, recess, and so on. As I was doing this, I realized that Ensley was left out of the conversation.

So I turned to her and said, "And you…you…where did you come from? Who are you? And what are you all about?"

Ensley looked up from her Cocoa Puffs and sat up straight in her chair with an appropriate expression of happy confusion on her face. She had no idea how to answer me, but she was glad to be a part of the conversation. I just stared right into her eyes and waited to see what she would say.

That's when Ace spoke up and said, "Hey, Dad…I hear that once you name them, YOU are responsible for them."

We all laughed together over that strange exchange of words, but I have never forgotten it. God spoke to me that morning

18

through my son. There is profound truth in knowing that once you name something you are responsible for it.

When you name your One, you become responsible for sharing Jesus with that person. There is a calling on your life to be Christ's ambassador to the person you are praying for. Just praying for that person becomes unsatisfactory. You will be compelled to take action. You will ask God to use you to share His love with them. You will go out of your way to spend time with them because you fully expect God to move in a mighty way at any moment.

You feel responsible, and it feels good. You are more than a recipient of Christ's Kingdom, you are a participant in building His Kingdom! The monotony of purposeless living is replaced with passionate responsibility. You will love like you have never loved before as Jesus reveals Himself through you. You will hurt for the person you are praying for. You will cry out to God with unparalleled passion. You will plead for them. You will be responsible.

Responsibility is a powerful thing.

When our youngest child, Ensley, started Kindergarten her brother Ace was in the second grade at the same school. The Kindergarten program was just a half-day and Ensley went to school in the afternoon. Each day, Ensley was dropped off at school just before noon and then she rode the bus home with her big brother when school was finished.

My wife and I were pretty nervous about our baby riding the bus home from school, so we appealed to her big brother Ace to be responsible for her. Ace is an amazing kid. He has a sweet spirit, and he loves his sisters. Ace is gentle, thoughtful, trustworthy, and compassionate…but at that time he was also an eight year old boy. We know that our son can be mischievous and a bit rotten at

19

times. He has that "Dennis the Menace" twinkle in his eyes. He is simultaneously endearing and alarming.

We are not the type of parents who pretend our kids are perfect. We have flawed children, and we like them that way. Stepford kids do not interest us in the least. Our kids have amazing personalities that we are responsible for cultivating. We try to set realistic expectations for them, and for the most part, they rise to the occasion, and sometimes they totally blow us away.

So there we were, Mom and Dad, nervous about our baby riding the bus home from school, so we called on the big brother to be responsible. We were not sure how Ace would respond, so we laid it on pretty thick. We told him to make sure his sister got on the right bus, that she was seated safely for the duration of the journey, and that she got off at the right stop. We explained to Ace that his baby sister could get lost, end up on the wrong bus, or be taken by a stranger.

Ace really seemed to understand the gravity of the situation and how much it meant to his mom and dad that he look out for his little sister. Before the first day of school, we showed Ace where the bus would drop them off. We walked him through how to tell the bus driver that they were together. When school finally started, Ace had a very clear mission, and he was up for the challenge.

It was a special moment, watching Ace and Ensley come off of the bus together on the first day of school. We were nervous, but our fears were put to rest when the bus pulled up and we saw Ace help his baby sister gather her belongings, and then he held her arm as she exited the bus. We were proud parents as they ran over to us to tell us all about their day.

Over the next couple of weeks, we reminded Ace to continue to make sure Ensley got on the right bus, but we were slipping into a routine. My wife and I weren't really nervous any longer. Ace had done a great job of helping his sister (and parents) adjust to a new situation. Everything was moving along normally, then one day something different happened.

I took Ace to school early one morning before going about my day. My wife woke up with a stomach bug and was unable to take Ensley to school. I was stuck in a meeting, so we decided to keep Ensley home. I was able to wrap things up early and went to the bus stop to pick up Ace. It was raining outside, so I waited for him in my car.

When the bus stopped, I saw Ace jump up immediately and head for the doors. He had a very serious look on his face. He locked eyes with me as he stepped off the bus, and he sprinted to my car. Ace threw open the back door and very sternly, seriously, and passionately told me what was going on.

He said, "Dad, Ensley was not on the bus. I don't know where she is. I couldn't find her, and I didn't know what to do. I don't know if she got on the wrong bus, if she is lost, or if someone took her. Dad, I don't know where Ensley is."

By the time he finished, his body was shaking and his lips were quivering. He was ghost-white with fear. Ace did not know where his baby sister was, and he felt responsible.

I reached toward him and said, "Oh, buddy, Ensley is at home. She is safe. Mom was sick today and couldn't take her to school. Ensley is waiting for you to come home and play with her."

Ace burst into tears as he climbed into the car. He sat in his seat and sobbed. Between sobs he said, "You should have told me. You should have let me know that Ensley wouldn't be on the bus."

I promised that we would never do that to him again. My gut was wrenching as I sat there with Ace thinking about what the last twenty minutes of his life were like. He rode that bus all that way home not knowing where his baby sister was. He did the only thing he knew to do. The first chance he had, he ran to his dad and told him that his One was lost.

I never want to forget that moment. There are so many people who are not on the bus yet. They are not safe at home with Jesus. They are lost.

And we are responsible.

It is that simple. Praying for One brings the reality of Christ's mission to your doorstep. When God gives you a name, you can't shake it. You become consumed with sharing God's love, and you plead with the Father for the lost to be found.

You cannot rationalize away your responsibility. You will not try to pass off your calling onto paid clergy members. You will stop making excuses. Your life will have purpose.

Once you name it, you are responsible for it. Pray for One, and go get them.

EXPERTLY
COMPLICATED

chapter three

EXPERTLY COMPLICATED

How did Christianity get so complicated?

Jesus entrusted His Church to a group of ordinary, unschooled people who believed so deeply in His mission that they died for Him. They were so busy sharing the simple gospel that there was no time to make it complex. The Lord was adding to their number daily those who were being saved.

Many subtle shifts have occurred over the centuries. Christianity became a state religion. It was organized. Church became big business. Power struggles ensued. The mission was sometimes lost.

But Jesus has never given up on His Church. He has bet all of eternity on the Church. We are His plan A, and there is no plan B. With all of our failings, the Church still prevails as the light of the world. Light is a very simple thing. It either shines or it doesn't. The same is true for the Church.

The light of the Church is shining brightly. Worldwide there are more people coming to know Jesus as Lord and Savior today than at any other time in history. The gospel is booming! The question we must wrestle with is: Are we a part of this explosion of light?

I am a pastor. I am a part of a system that can profit from making simple truths complex. I admit that I have desired to be a part of the system of "religious experts." I have tried to finagle my way into the club, but one requirement continually trips me up. I can't get my head around taking the simple truth of Jesus and making it inaccessible to others. The whole notion of "religious experts" runs contrary to the beauty of the gospel.

Seriously? Religious experts? What does that even mean?

Do you want to know who the real religious experts are in practicing true religion? It is not necessarily the highly-educated, professional clergy, authors, speakers, and pop-culture Jesus icons. The religious experts are the ones who excel at taking care of orphans and widows in their distress. Religious experts have a childlike faith that is accompanied by obedient action. Experts in following Jesus demonstrate their faith in abiding love for God that is reproduced exponentially as they generously share the hope that they possess.

The church I serve with is in Manchester, New Hampshire. We have some of the greatest religious experts I have ever encountered. The people of Manchester Christian Church pray for One, and that simple prayer has driven them to deep action. There was a small group of people in our church that became aware of a problem in our city. On Saturdays and Sundays, there were no shelters or services providing breakfast for our homeless neighbors. Their love for Jesus compelled them to act.

Once they recognized the need, they began showing up at a downtown park with breakfast foods. They shared a meal, a devotional thought, and the love of Jesus with anyone who wanted to join them. Initially, they served a "cold" breakfast, but they were not content with that. The Holy Spirit stirred within them to give their best, so they began to cook hot, delicious food. Word spread quickly.

They created a ministry named "Do You Know Him?" because their ultimate goal is for everyone to know Jesus. In less than one year, the ministry grew to over 150 regular volunteers who help serve hundreds of people each Saturday and Sunday morning. People aren't just eating a meal, they are being saved.

An older lady who helped start the ministry came up to me one Sunday and said, "Oh, honey, I prayed for ONE and got 22. What do I do now?" I replied, "Well, what do you want to do?" She looked at me with tears in her eyes and a grin on her face and said, "I want to pray for another One!"

This ministry changed the complexion of our church as our doors were suddenly thrown open to an entirely new demographic of people. The social, economic, and racial diversity is beautiful. We worship together. We serve together. We laugh together. We cry together. Most importantly, we are together. There is no "us" and "them"...it's all us. We are Manchester Christian Church.

Our church has grown so much that, out of necessity, we opened new campuses. We ran out of seats. There was nowhere left to put people. We started a beautiful new campus downtown that is within walking distance from the park where breakfast is served. Now everyone can come without having to catch a ride. But our Downtown Campus is not a homeless church. It is Manchester

Christian Church. It is that same beautiful mixture of people. We are experiencing heaven on earth.

This is what happens when you move beyond the academics of Christianity and into the reality of being a disciple of Jesus. Discipleship is simple, but simple does not mean shallow. In fact, the simplest things are often the deepest. Our religious experts pray for One and are radically obedient to the mission of Christ. The world is in desperate need of more people who are experts in true religion.

A religious expert is really just a disciple, and a disciple is really just a follower of Jesus. What do followers of Jesus do? They do what Jesus did. Jesus was asked why He came to earth, and He replied, "The Son of Man came to seek and save the lost."

The professional Christian community is perpetually tempted to promote myths regarding discipleship. Complexity creates job security because people must rely on experts to instruct them. The average churchgoer has no hope of interpreting the intricate system of expectations and regulations that are invented by men. The burden of the complex system proves to be too much as the weight of law crushes people and prevents them from following Jesus. What remains is a stagnant mess of defeated despair.

Everyone who receives the good news of Jesus starts out the same. We want to share His extraordinary love with others. We want more people in the Kingdom of Heaven, but then something happens. We hit a snag. There's a bump in the road. There's push back and spiritual attack. Without realizing it, we adjust our initial aim and shoot for something that produces less resistance.

These new goals and objectives are usually good and often even noble. They are easy to support from scripture. Churchy people like the sound of them and eagerly nod their approval. They gain traction quickly and produce a minor spark of life and hope.

The problem with these new goals is that they are not what Jesus called us to do. We share in His mission, and when Jesus was asked what He came here to do, He did not mince any words. Jesus said that the Son of Man came to seek and save the lost. So if a church is not seeking and saving the lost, it is not fulfilling the mission of Jesus and, by definition, is not a church.

The temptation is to throw around weird little phrases like, "We are equipping the saints." Ok, but what in the world are you equipping the saints to do? It better be to seek and save the lost because that is what Jesus commanded. What good are more saintly saints if they aren't fulfilling the mission of Jesus? They are no good. They are a waste of Jesus with skin on. What good are they serving if Jesus is not actively demonstrating His love through them? Jesus warned us that fruitless branches would be cut off.

What are Christians?

They are resources.

Resources for what?

To seek and save the lost!

To live is Christ, and to die is gain. If we live, it is to carry out the purpose of Jesus' life on earth. We will have an eternity to worship Jesus and to know Him fully, but the here and now is the only opportunity we have to seek and save the lost. We don't get to do that in eternity, so we better leverage every resource at our disposal right now to make sure that every single lost one is found. We do not rest, stop, or pause until the mission is complete.

Some will argue that we are out of our minds. BINGO! We are out of our minds for Christ. We are starting to get over personal agendas, insecurities, and selfishness. Love us. Hate us.

31

We don't care. We just want you to love Jesus and snatch others from the eternal fire of Hell.

Some will say that we are too focused on evangelism. Think about that for a minute. Seriously consider the implications of that statement. How can Christ's Church ever be too focused on His mission? It is absurd to think that we could ever go overboard when it comes to seeking and saving the lost.

On Judgment Day, I can't imagine Jesus condemning us for trying too hard to seek the lost. I doubt that we will be chastised for lovingly proclaiming the beauty of the simple gospel with focused clarity instead of muddling through confusion-invoking studies on irrelevant subject matter.

Some may say, "Well, it is Jesus who saves, not us."

True, but what exactly do you think that the Church is? We are the body of Christ. We are His physical presence here on earth. It is extremely difficult to philosophize and explain away the Great Commission.

The apostles and the early Church gave their lives for the simple gospel. Persecution and the critical nature of the mission prevented perverting the gospel with false notions of easy living or new and improved strands of legalism. Seeking and saving the lost was paramount. That simple mission remains, and the Church must take hold of it.

Do you want to see a change? Pray for One, and watch what happens. Nothing remains the same when we pray for One. I believe with all my heart that one simple prayer can change the landscape of the modern church, the world, and your life.

"God, please give me One person to share your love with today. Amen."

THE COST OF FREE

chapter four

THE COST OF FREE

Grace is free, but discipleship will cost you everything.

Identity is the only thing of value that we possess.

Money is an illusion. It's just a bunch of made up numbers. None of it is real. Each month numbers show up in the bank account, then they go away. Hope in economic security is about as real as sitting on a cloud.

Possessions have zero eternal value. They will all pass away. The heavens and the earth will all disappear. Along with your house, car, golf clubs, clothes, and jewelry. If you try to hold onto them, you'll just share in their destruction.

Families fail. Divorce, death, and dysfunction destroy families. If your family is your ultimate, you will ultimately be disappointed.

The only thing Jesus wants is you.

Jesus calls us to be His disciples, but discipleship is one of those churchy words that gets manipulated and twisted in all sorts of deceptive ways. Discipleship often gets relegated into classes and programs that focus on knowledge transference.

The general thinking is that the more we learn, the more we will be like Jesus. Practical experience should have demolished this myth long ago, but we still gladly replace following Jesus with biblical stuffiness. The Bible is abused like food for a glutton. Instead of fuel for the mission, the scriptures become addictive junk food. The Bible is abused like a drug as we grow puffed up, lethargic, and obese. The mission of following Jesus gets replaced with the drive to be smarter than the rest.

We are forced to turn inward in efforts to justify the absence of evangelistic traction. Instead of talking about, dreaming of, and praying over people getting saved, we argue about petty nuances of scripture that are largely irrelevant. Christians divide over the ridiculous. The Bible is used as a weapon against one another instead of as a sword to set the captives free.

Don't get me wrong. I love the Bible. I read it every day. I preach from it every Sunday. I memorize scripture, and I encourage everyone to seek Jesus in all sixty-six wonderful books.

But, I do not worship the Bible. I worship Jesus. Discipleship is following Jesus.

We cannot replace following Jesus with following the Bible. In order for the Bible to be useful for discipleship, it must be read through the lens of Jesus. We must consider who Jesus is and His mission before we can appropriately apply scripture to daily living. If we fail to do this, then scripture will be taken out of context and abused for whatever purpose we deem desirable.

At the extreme level, you can picture those protesters that we have all seen on television holding up signs that say things like "God hates fags." Those devils are the worst kind of Antichrist. They misrepresent who Jesus is because of a perverted agenda. But is it possible that we participate in the same kind of activity every time we use the Bible for something other than an encounter with the living, loving Jesus?

Hopefully the thought of misrepresenting Jesus to this lost, broken, and devastated world disturbs you greatly. My heart breaks over the vast amount of resources that are wasted on false discipleship efforts. The enemy's number one tactic is to get the Church to focus on anything other than the mission of Jesus. If he can get us to fight on a false front, then he wins the battle no matter how valiantly or powerfully we struggle. Fighting the wrong fight is actually worse than not fighting at all.

For years now, I have read books and listened to Christian leaders discuss and debate over what authentic discipleship looks like. I have encountered countless discipleship models, programs, and strategies. They all seek to create a measurable system where growth can be documented and compared. We have complicated the simplest of concepts in attempts to control and contain what can only be a dynamic experience. Discipleship is not something you can conquer and graduate from. It is a journey that leads into eternity. We do not arrive as disciples of Jesus until we fall at His feet at judgment and experience His refining fire once and for all.

We must refrain from removing the mystery and wonder of following Jesus. It is a glorious thing to stumble after the Messiah. The Bible is full of flawed people who pursued God and sometimes succeeded but often failed. Discipleship is nothing other than following Jesus and doing what He did.

Jesus was crystal clear on what following Him would look like. The central components of His teachings reveal three indicative marks that every follower of Christ will exhibit. Authentic disciples love God, love people, and reproduce spiritually. These are the marks of Kingdom-minded men and women. They are consumed with love and purpose. The allure of this world and the distractions of self are no match for the compelling nature of following hard after Jesus. Authentic disciples have tasted the heavenly gift of living beyond this realm, and there is no satisfaction in the purely temporal.

When Jesus was asked what the greatest commandment is, He replied: "Love the Lord your God with all your heart, soul, mind, and strength." Love is discipleship fuel. When someone is connected to God through a relationship with Jesus, they are able to receive and reciprocate love. The love of God is more than the human heart can contain, so it bursts out and overflows in a sort of love explosion.

The most important thing is to love God with every fiber of your being. Hold nothing back. Nothing is off limits to Him. You are to love God with all of your heart, soul, mind, and strength. This reveals to us the all-encompassing nature of discipleship. There are no partial disciples. Either you are all in, or you aren't in at all. This notion ought to disturb and shake us at our very core. Christianity is not a child's play thing. Jesus is not to be toyed with. The thought of merely playing follow the leader with Jesus until we become bored, tired, afraid, or irritated is a vulgar concept indeed!

There are no vacations from discipleship. We are never on a break from God. Compartmentalization is a lie. Thinking that we can effectively follow Jesus in one area of our life while deliberately disobeying Him in another area is insane. We attempt to barter and compromise, but God does not compromise. His terms are clear. Love Him with everything you have.

Our God is a jealous God. He will not share us. He is unwilling to accept idolatry. We can get sucked into the vicious world of idolatry without much awareness at all. Our idols are often good things that become supreme things. We put them ahead of God and allow them to dictate our thoughts and actions. Family, work, recreation, health, prosperity, nationalism, humanistic endeavors, and so on, can easily become the primary filters that drive our lives.

The command to love the Lord your God with all of your heart, soul, mind, and strength does not allow for any form of idolatry. God is faithful in this command by allowing us to receive salvation with our whole being. Acts 2 recounts the story of the first time the gospel of Jesus was shared with a group of people. Their response is telling.

When they heard the message of Jesus, they were cut to the heart and said, "What must we do to be saved?" Peter replied, "Repent and be baptized, every one of you, in the name of Jesus Christ for the forgiveness of your sins."

Salvation is a holistic experience.

The people heard the story of Jesus and were cut to the heart. The love of God hit them at their core. This is the initial response to an awareness of God's intense love for us. We receive it in our hearts, and the heart/soul cannot contain it. We are compelled to action because the love of God requires release.

The people asked, "What must we do to be saved?"

For the sake of a theological side note, it is important to state that salvation is not initiated by our actions. Ephesians 2:8-10 reminds us that, "For it is by grace you have been saved, through faith—and this not from yourselves, it is the gift of God— not by works, so that no one can boast. For we are God's workmanship, created in Christ Jesus to do good works, which God prepared in advance for us to do."

I have no desire to get sidetracked by a debate regarding the nature of grace and works in the salvation process. I would also prefer to avoid triggering the various defenses about what is required for salvation. For the most part, that discussion simply detracts from the beauty of Christ's redemptive work. Attempts to ascertain the bare minimum requirements for salvation reveal a lack of understanding of lordship. Salvation is only found through Jesus being Lord. If Jesus is Lord, then obedience will follow. Salvation opens the door for obedience to all of God's commands through a relationship with Jesus. The truly saved person has no reason to balk at any of God's commands.

So, back to the question that was asked in Acts chapter 2. "What must we do to be saved?"

The Apostle Peter replied, "Repent and be baptized, every one of you, in the name of Jesus Christ for the forgiveness of your sins."

Already, they were cut to the heart. The jealous love of God was pounding on and in their hearts and souls. They were desperate to respond, and Peter told them to do two things.

The first was to repent. Receiving grace, forgiveness, and salvation all begins with one of the greatest words ever…Repent. Repentance is far more than feeling bad or sorry for sinning. It is more than making a commitment to try not to sin anymore. Repentance entails a completely fresh and new start. It is a choice to have your entire worldview changed.

Romans 12:2 says, "Be transformed by the renewing of

your mind." Repentance means that we get to live for God instead of anything else. Repentance means that the number one, most important thing in our lives is our relationship with God. Repentance means that we are restored to the place God intended for us to be from the beginning…to an interdependent relationship with our loving Creator.

The new way of thinking that comes from repentance provides a fresh outlook on life as we experience the love of God with our minds. The only way to love God with all your mind is through repentance. We take captive every thought and make it obedient to Christ by filtering it through an eternal view of salvation. As this occurs, our internal dialogue begins to change. Our passions, desires, and dreams are altered by a radically different vision of what the future holds. We start to want what God wants as our minds are captured by His graceful promptings. The temporal loses its grip as our thoughts are consumed with matters of eternal significance.

The second way Peter told them to respond was to be baptized. Baptism is the physical experience connected to the emotional and mental surrender to Jesus. The command to be baptized should not be surprising. Jesus was baptized. He commanded His disciples to "go and baptize." There is no reason for anyone who has been cut to the heart with the gospel and is experiencing the transforming of the mind through repentance not to be baptized.

Sadly though, baptism has landed on the denominational battle lines. It has been fought over, abused, neglected, and misrepresented for centuries. The mere mention of it causes some to shut down completely.

It saddens me greatly when baptism is argued about and debated. I believe that we clearly have missed the entire point of baptism when it becomes little more than a "doctrinal issue" that must be proved. I have never once met a Christ-follower who refused baptism after hearing about the true beauty of the sacred experience. I have, however, met many who, after taking their doctrinal beating, refused baptism because it had become merely a theological point to be proved.

Baptism is one of God's greatest gifts to His children. It is commanded clearly in scripture and was part of the normative conversion/initiation practice in the early Church. That alone should be sufficient reason to be baptized. The issue generally becomes contentious when we discuss what actually occurs at the point of baptism.

Does the Holy Spirit come at baptism? Does salvation occur at baptism? Are sins washed away at baptism?

The point is not to understand fully what transpires at baptism but to respond in obedience to the command. In the book of Acts, we see several different conversion experiences with different things happening at different times. This leads to some of the confusion and provides ammunition for the doctrinal debate. The debates are a distraction from the beauty of the gift of baptism. The fact is that God has commanded baptism, and lordship demands obedience. If we refuse to obey this simple command, then how in the world could we possibly believe that we will be ready for the more challenging elements of following Jesus?

This is typically one of the first steps of obedience in a Christ-follower's life, but many times it is not taught. People simply do not know that baptism is what God desires. Often days, months, and years can go by before this command is pointed out. Unfortunately, baptism then can become a barrier instead of a blessing. People may want to prove that they are "okay" without it or that it is not "necessary" for salvation. Arguing these points often causes hardened hearts to become harder.

It is essential that we teach the true beauty of baptism. Baptism is a gift from God. God wants us to experience Him completely, with our entire being. We receive His love and grace when the Word or gospel message penetrates our hearts. We also experience God's grace with our minds as they are transformed and renewed. God is not satisfied with that though. He wants us to experience this salvation completely.

That includes experiencing His salvation with our bodies. God gives us baptism so that we can enter into His death, burial, and resurrection with every part of who we are, from our hearts to our minds, from our heads to our toes. It is a complete and total experience that entails a complete and total transformation. We become completely God's...mind, body, and soul.

Why would anyone refuse that?

So love the Lord with all of your heart, soul, mind and strength. Love Him with everything you've got. Hold nothing back. The greatest command is holistic in nature. It leaves no wiggle room.

Jesus wants all of you, and He will not settle for less. Jesus came and gave His life as a ransom to redeem you. Salvation is a free gift from God, but it will cost you everything to receive this gift. You will spend your life on something. Why not spend it on what you were created for? Grace is free, but discipleship will cost you your life.

"Then he said to them all: 'If anyone would come after me, he must deny himself and take up his cross daily and follow me. For whoever wants to save his life will lose it, but whoever loses his life for me will save it.'"
Luke 9:23-24

45

Praying for One is a way to lay down your life every day. Put your agenda aside to take up the mission of Jesus.

"Yes, Lord, give me One!"

ONE PRAYER
DOES IT ALL

chapter five

ONE PRAYER DOES IT ALL

Discipleship is not a linear process. There have been many great attempts to create forms of systematic discipleship. They provide step-by-step manuals for following Jesus. Do this. Take this class. Then take the next class. Join a group. Participate in an outreach event. Witness to a friend. Practice spiritual disciplines. Read this. Pray that. Now hang your certificate on the wall. And POOF! You are a bona fide follower of Jesus.

Discipleship just doesn't work that way.

Following Jesus is an organic process. It is full of life. Every gut-wrenching stumble in His direction reveals that discipleship is a journey and not a destination. You never arrive at discipleship. It is not something to complete or conquer.

This is a significant problem in churches today. Several generations have graduated from discipleship programs and have sufficiently lost the wonder of following Jesus. They completed the system and came out on the other side of discipleship. Now what?

What happens when you are taught to follow a process instead of Jesus? What do you do when the process ends?

We don't need another system. We don't need more hurdles to clear. We don't need more achievement. We just need Jesus. We are desperate for Jesus. We need His love to flow through us to this broken world and to reflect back to the Father. Nothing less will do.

Followers of Jesus do the three things that are commanded in the Great Commandment and the Great Commission. They love God, love people, and make more disciples.

If you genuinely pray for One, all three of these things will happen. It is impossible to pray earnestly for One and not love God, love people, and reproduce spiritually.

Connect to God

Asking God to give you One person to share His love with connects you to the very heartbeat of Jesus. When we want what Jesus wants, we begin to love Him with unparalleled passion. If you really want your relationship with God to grow, then throw yourself into what He is excited about.

Most of the time we pray to convince God to do our will. We beg and plead for Him to intervene and make everything just the way we want it. In essence, when we pray this way, we are asking God to make us the center of the universe. We want people to serve us, circumstances to favor us, and God to obey us.

After all, we are entitled, right? We completed the program. We did the steps. We did our part. Now where is that magically perfect life we were promised? I want my dream life now, and I want it on my terms because I know best!

Ugh. My heart aches. How many prayers have I wasted on me? How many requests had nothing to do with following Jesus? How many have revealed the discipleship lies I so eagerly clung to? My idolatrous prayers of self-promotion left me further from Jesus than I ever imagined possible.

It is impossible to follow Jesus when your primary concern is self. Every form of prosperity preaching is an abomination, but the more subtle versions are the most dangerous.

Sure, we can turn on the television and laugh at ridiculous rants of the phony "give to get" messengers. We spot them and scoff at their unenlightened, Antichrist verbiage. The chuckles turn to irritation as we shake condescending heads in disgust and change the channel.

We change the channel, but the encounter is not over. The message lingers. Our laughter and irritation converge into a sick sense of pride. It is easy to mock the far end of the prosperity spectrum while allowing the same seeds of deception to blossom in our hearts. We compare ourselves to the thieving preachers on TV and in doing so readily accept the more subtle principles of greed, selfishness, and idolatry.

There is a steady line of thinking within mainstream Christianity that promotes the premise that if we are good little boys and girls, then nothing bad will ever happen to us. Following Jesus is taught as a safe way for the entire family to experience prosperity, health, and the American Dream. Discipleship is twisted as the aim is shifted from building God's Kingdom to enhancing each individual's kingdom. When the primary concern is how the individual benefits from following Christ, the ultimate goal of discipleship is utterly lost.

Disciples have a functional goal…to make more disciples.

There is no such thing as discipleship without the end result being more disciples. The "mile wide and inch deep" arguments are ridiculous. Authentic discipleship is always deep and wide. Quality disciples will produce more disciples.

Numbers matter. Reproduction matters. People being saved matters. Jesus didn't die so that His Church could sit around in holy huddles comparing their knowledge of scripture against one another. Jesus didn't die so that His Church could lead comfortable lives based on the notion that God's primary concern is to make us happy. Jesus did not die so that His Church could ignore His chief concern…to seek and save the lost.

Pray for One, and people will be saved. Pray for One, and God will answer. Pray for One, and exponential growth will become reality.

An important way to measure quality is through the increase in quantity. Disciples make more disciples. It is what we do. If we do not make more disciples, then something is tragically wrong.

Seriously, this is just simple logic. If the point of Christianity is only to become more "Jesus-ly" then wouldn't it make way more sense to die now? Let's all just die and appear before Christ at judgment where every impurity will be burned away in an instant. We have been justified through Christ, so let's go ahead and skip out on the painful process of sanctification. What's the point of living and being sanctified if it is not for the mission of Jesus? Christ's Church is here on earth to seek and save the lost.

So do we seek Jesus, grow in our devotion to Him, read the Bible daily, give generously, serve faithfully, participate in small groups, learn, obey, and so on? Of course!

But why?

The foundational reason for doing all the things that we call discipleship is for the purpose of making more disciples. The more we love Jesus, the more we will love His mission. The more we become like Jesus, the more people will be saved because we lay down our lives and take up our crosses to follow Him. The more sacrificial we become, the more we will live to build Christ's eternal Kingdom and the less concern we will have for the temporary things of this world.

Praying for One flips a switch.

It takes the focus off of all things me and puts the focus on all things Jesus. Discipleship is an all Jesus, all the time reality. Praying for One connects us to the heartbeat of Jesus.

Praying for One is a bit painful at first, because you become keenly aware of what you have been praying for. When you begin praying for One, start by taking captive every thought in prayer and make it obedient to Christ. When I did this, I realized that the vast majority of my prayers where about irrelevant things. Praying for personal success, protection, and prosperity was not connecting me to the love of God…it was merely reinforcing my love of self.

I began to replace my prayers for self with prayers for One. I would ramble on honestly about whatever personal concern I had, and then I would say, "But what I really want is One person to share your love with."

The prayers for One steadily became more prevalent as concern for self began to dwindle. The passion that comes from escaping the prison of self and being free to pursue the mission of Christ is impossible to explain. You must experience it for yourself.

Praying for One sets your heart in rhythm with the heartbeat of Jesus. Christianity is a miserable thing indeed when we are out of step with Jesus. There is confusion, doubt, deceit, irritation, conflict, dissension, and the like, when our passion does not match Christ's.

It is impossible to pray earnestly for One and not love God more. When you share His heart, you see even deeper into His love, and that love will explode within you. Our best expression of love to the Father is to do what He commands us to do. Praying for One sets our feet on the path of obedience because concern for self is no longer primary.

Connect to People

So the Great Commandment is to love God with everything you've got, and the second is like it...to love your neighbor as yourself. Do you think that praying for One will help in that whole "loving your neighbor" thing?

When you pray for One, you can't help but love your neighbor. Praying for One establishes you as a love conduit. God's love begins to flow through you to everyone you are connected to. When you make yourself available to God in this fashion, He will place people directly in your path for the purpose of sharing His love.

God's will is that none should perish. God's plan is to use you to extend His grace to others. You are plan A, and there is no plan B. If you refuse to allow God's love to move through you to others, then they will not know the reality of the gospel. Praying for One opens up the floodgates of love and exposes people to the refreshing current of God's mercy.

Praying for One is a perfectly logical way to respond to the salvation and calling of Jesus. Christians are always clamoring on about seeking God's will. The Kingdom of Heaven would be way better off if we stopped asking the same question over and over again and simply accepted the answer God has given. God's will is obvious. Make disciples.

The only way to become confused is to make this complex. We often make this complex to find justification for fruitless living. There is no justification for fruitless living. Either you are making disciples, or you are not. Either you are living for Jesus, or you are not. Either Jesus is Lord, or you are lost.

When you pray for One, God says, "YES!"

This can be the boldest prayer you've ever prayed because it is one that can be expressed with extreme confidence. There is no mystery here. When you ask God to give you One to share His love with, how do you think He will respond?

God's not going to say, "Well, isn't that sweet? I appreciate your willingness to help out, but I've got this one all taken care of. You've done enough already. Heaven's got plenty of people. I don't really care about those who don't know me. We will go ahead and let them experience eternal separation from me. Instead of sharing my love, why don't you just hoard it and allow it to fester in your heart? That way you can be spoiled rotten from the inside out and become repulsive instead of attractive to those who do not know me."

God says yes to our prayers for One because His love must be shared. His love is a fresh commodity. If you hold it in your heart instead of releasing it to others, His love will rot.

There really is nothing more disgusting than a spoiled Christian. When God's love is not released, there is a sickening turn inward. We begin to consider every thought through the filter of self instead of through the mission of Christ. The inward turn plunges us in a downward descent of depravity. It throws the door open for the most dangerous of all sins...self-righteousness.

Praying for One removes the focus from self and places it squarely on building Christ's Kingdom. We are inspired to a noble cause and are able to transcend self in an upward capacity.

Following Jesus is the liberation from self. We escape the torment of being our own god. We become a part of building His eternal Kingdom instead of merely tinkering in our private affairs. Life only makes sense when it is lived in the context of eternity. Eternity only holds hope when it is viewed in the context of Jesus. Jesus only changes us when He is truly Lord. Lordship only occurs through total surrender. Surrender can only happen when we are willing to abandon self.

When pleas for One become your ultimate prayer, you are set free from the bondage of self and can truly love your neighbor. It is fantastic. This is the expressed will of God. He will answer your prayers for One with a resounding, "YES!"

It's kind of like a teenager asking his mom if it would be okay if he cleaned his room. How's mom going to respond to that question? Her initial reaction may be to faint, but after she is revived the answer will be "Yes!" "Yes, son, you may clean your room. What do you need in order to do a good job? Is there a way that I can help you? Thank you for participating in my mission to maintain our home."

God will use you if you let Him. God will transform you if you allow Him. God will love people through you if you are open to Him. The heart change that comes as a result of praying for One radically alters your worldview. People are no longer irritations to be avoided; they are opportunities to be experienced.

God wants people in this world to know how much they are loved, and His Church is the chosen vehicle for delivering His love. God loves people through us, but we must be available, alert, and aggressive with His love. The love of God is not some kind of non-renewable resource that needs to be hoarded in case of shortages.

Love grows as it is shared. The only time that it is in short supply is when it is blockaded within the human heart. Try to hold God's love inside by refusing to share it, and the ceaseless flow is dammed. Open the floodgates by praying for One, and the refreshing flow of God's grace, mercy, and love rushes over the parched and desperate land. The dead are brought to life. The weary are refreshed. His love heals, restores, and revives.

God's love is sufficient, but only if it is shared. People need to be touched by the love of God. The real-world experience of receiving love is not a mystical connection with an undefined source. God puts a face to love by using His people.

Praying for One makes us an extension of God's love. It's kind of like an electrical power strip. We plug into the source by connecting to God and receiving His love. Then we plug into others so that the love of God is channeled through us to them. Then they plug into others and to others and to others until the whole world is connected to the eternal source of authentic love.

When you pray for One, a switch gets flipped in your heart. There is a change in purpose. You begin to look at people differently. There is an expectation that every encounter is an opportunity for God's love to be experienced through you. In the middle of casual conversations, you will be struck by the reality that "this could be my One."

You will find yourself praying ceaselessly in the midst of everyday life for wisdom, courage, and compassion. People will see something different in you, and they will expose themselves in surprising ways. You will be in over your head. Human wisdom will not suffice. You will be forced to depend on the power of the Holy Spirit dwelling within you. It can be a terrifying thing, but when you yield to God's love, His truth will rush out of you and wash over others.

Praying for One moves us beyond the placating lies of our cultural norms and into the raw and authentic truth. When you pray for One, loving truth begins to pour out of you into others. The authenticity of God's love is thoroughly disarming. People are so used to being lied to that when they hear loving truth, they stop dead in their tracks.

I once encountered a man after one of our worship services who was visibly shaken by what he had just experienced. He came out of the auditorium before the service was over. The lobby was fairly empty, and I was sitting on a stool off to the side. As he got closer to me, I could see the mixture of emotion in his face. There was fear, anger, doubt, despair, grief, and guilt. The flood of emotion was more than he could handle, and tears began to stream down his weathered cheeks.

I leaned forward and made eye contact with him. I asked if he was okay, and he responded, "No." I asked what was going on, and he told me that he had never experienced anything like our church. He said that the presence of God was undeniable, and he knew that he needed God's love, but he said he couldn't stay. When I asked why he couldn't stay, his voice faltered and cracked as he barely breathed the words, "I'm not worthy."

My initial reaction was to say, "Yes, you are. You are worthy. Don't leave." I opened my mouth, but the look on his face was too real for me to spin some kind of condescending lie. He knew he was not worthy, and so did I.

The look on my face was sufficient truth for him, and he gave a simple nod and began to walk away. In my spirit, I was crying out to God. In that instant, I loved this man in a way that I will never be able to explain. I prayed, "Help me God," as I watched the man walking away.

Then without thinking, I stood and yelled, "STOP!" Everyone in the lobby froze. The man turned and looked at me. He was defeated and done, but there was a flicker of hope deep within his eyes. This was a holy moment.

I pointed at him and excitedly said, "Neither am I."

Those words of simple truth hit him like a surge of electricity. His countenance changed, and he moved toward me. I put my hand on his shoulder, and I told him the truth, "I'm not worthy either. None of us are. We all need grace."

Praying for One frees you to love people with truth. The awareness that comes from expecting God to answer your most passionate plea sets your mind ready for action. In the moment of truth...when your One is standing before you...your soul will leap with anticipation over what God is about to do.

His love is contagious. It spreads like wildfire. God's love moves through a gentle touch, an encouraging word, an act of kindness, a generous gesture, and the like. God works through the simple and uses the available. That's the beauty of praying for One. Simply put, it makes you available.

Connect to Mission

Every person you encounter is a potential One. Every appointment is divine. Every conversation is a unique opportunity to share God's love. Every day has a purpose, and each moment is filled with mission.

When you awake each morning with a prayer for One on your lips, there is no confusion about what the day will hold. The gospel is each day's destination. It doesn't matter where you go or what you do...the end result is still the same...people are going to be saved!

Please understand this. If you pray for One, people will be saved. God will use you. He will say "Yes" to your predominant prayer.

God will use YOU. The prevailing attitude is that God only uses pastors and religious leaders for this sort of thing, but the truth of the matter is that pastors are the most likely to mess this up. We complicate things. We overthink things. We rationalize and justify. We philosophize and theorize. We get hung up on theological concepts and question everything. We get paralyzed in the minutia.

Just pray for One, and then get your head out of the sand. That's our biggest problem on the missional front...we bury our heads in the sand and pretend that the lost are not a reality. One of the greatest barriers to evangelism is that many Christians will claim that they do not know any lost people. I'm not buying that, and neither should you.

Pull your head out, and take a look around. Pray for One, and God will place people directly in your path. Lost people are everywhere. They live in your neighborhood, work in your office, exercise at your gym, wait on your table, teach your kids, pick up your trash, deliver your mail, treat your illnesses, and so on.

The problem with our thinking is the word "your" in the previous sentence. We tend to view people as being in our world, on our turf, for the purpose of meeting our needs. If you are a Christian, this is not your world. You are a stranger and an alien here. You have a heavenly home. Our time on this planet is to be spent intentionally serving as ambassadors for our eternal home.

Egocentrism places self at the center of an individual's universe and assumes that everything else will revolve around and support the all-important core. All emphasis is placed on "me" as life is carried out in a series of self-serving events. This inward focus slams tight the door to the prison of self and intense sadness consumes the inmate. Desperate longing ensues as no satisfaction can be found. We are compelled to transcend self, but we do not know how.

Initial attempts to escape the prison of self are often spent in humanitarian efforts. This parallel transcendence of self produces momentary feelings of satisfaction as we seek to meet the needs of others. Our "good deeds" feel good indeed, but they are not good enough.

It doesn't take long to realize that the needs are greater than we can meet. With every act of kindness comes the recognition that our human efforts are insufficient. We cannot do enough. We serve one, and there are one hundred more whose needs go unmet. The unfairness of life overwhelms. Our good deeds are met with resistance, and positive efforts can even produce negative results. Those we help take advantage of us, turn on us, reject us, and punish us.

Frustration sets in and drives us deeper into the depths of self with even more intense feelings of sadness and hopelessness. We lose faith in our fellow humans and rightly so. People disappoint because they are flawed. They are not worthy of our faith any more than we are worthy of theirs. Humanitarian efforts without divine intervention do nothing for the long-term escape from self.

I certainly am not proposing that we not serve others. The point is that serving others is only effective in the long run if it points both the server and the one being served toward relationship with Jesus. Self-generated efforts always lead to a deeper turn inwards.

Another way that we attempt to escape self is through downward transcendence. Most often this is expressed through self-destructive behaviors. Addiction, abuse, and indulgence in sin create a temporary euphoria, but the momentary escape carries a hefty price. Guilt, shame, paranoia, and the fixation with finding the next fix overwhelm.

Attempts to escape self through descending behaviors will ultimately result in destruction. Pleasure seeking outside of a relationship with Jesus plunges us into a type of solitary confinement. This adds loneliness to the previously mentioned sadness and hopelessness.

Parallel and downward transcendence of self only serve to make matters worse, but there is another option. We can transcend self upwardly through a relationship with God. When this occurs, every notion of self is replaced with Lordship. God provides purpose, meaning, hope, happiness, satisfaction, pleasure, and all things good.

God uses us to serve others, but our efforts always point to Him. This mitigates the problems with parallel transcendence because God is capable of meeting all needs. We are not overwhelmed with the unfairness of this world because our focus is out of this world. People can still reject, abuse, and punish us, but what does that matter? We are no longer our own. We serve another. Self no longer has power to control, so things that would have previously impacted us negatively are rendered impotent.

Upward transcendence opens the door for ultimate soul satisfaction. We are free to experience pleasure through relationship with Jesus. Be warned...addiction is a virtual guarantee, but it is the best kind of addiction. When you pray for One, intense pleasure is experienced every time God provides another to share His love with. I have never met anyone who prayed for One, got One, and then thought that One was enough.

One is never enough! Praying for One is addictive in the purest sense. It will take over every aspect of your life as you are consumed with the mission of Jesus to seek and save the lost. Upward transcendence through praying for One destroys sadness, hopelessness, and loneliness because we are consumed with building into God's eternal Kingdom. This is the only valid escape from the prison of self.

The Great Commandment of loving God and loving others provides the fuel for living out the Great Commission of making disciples. When you love God, you must love others because you are connected to the source of love, and it must flow through you. When you love others, you must share Jesus with them because love requires action.

Love is not passive. It is not passive-aggressive. It is aggressive-aggressive.

Authentic followers of Christ are compelled to action. They are sucked into the divine fray. It is impossible to be a passive spectator in the Kingdom-building work of Jesus. When you belong to Him, you become much more than a recipient of grace... you become a participant in grace.

65

Others will experience God's eternal power and divine nature through you as Jesus makes Himself known in you. Christ's Church is His physical presence on earth, and He makes His appeal through us. He reconciles humankind to Himself, and Christians are entrusted with the ministry of reconciliation.

We are God's plan A, and there is no plan B.

When we refuse to participate in His mission, people are not saved. There is gravity to this gut-wrenching truth that must capture our attention and move us to drastic action. We are responsible.

Yes…Jesus does the redemptive work, but we share in this work. We know that salvation can only come through Jesus, but the message must come through His Body. Jesus took sin inside of Himself, put it to death on the cross, and conquered death through His resurrection. Sin remained dead, but He is alive. Eternal life is found only through sharing in His resurrection.

We are created in God's image for the purpose of partnership. The first command God gave Adam and Eve was to be fruitful and multiply. That same command applies today. We must be fruitful and multiply. Praying for One sets our course in this direction and maintains consistent and steady aim.

How do we know if we are successful in life? We are only successful if the Creator's purpose is fulfilled in us. His purpose is for us to partner with Him in His work. Are more people in the Kingdom of Heaven because of how God uses you? This really is the only question that matters.

Pray for One, and your aim will be right. You can't hit what you don't aim for. People do not just accidentally fall into discipleship. Discipleship occurs through concerted effort and prayerful devotion.

Disciples do what Jesus did. What did Jesus do? He made disciples. Disciples make disciples. Period.

If you are not reproducing spiritually, then you are not a disciple of Jesus. There is no way around this simple logic. The plain truth is before us. How will we respond?

My response is to pray for One because when I pray for One, people are saved. I love God more. I love people more. I love Christ's mission more. One prayer does it all.

CHURCH IN 3D

chapter six

CHURCH IN 3D

One of the greatest issues that many Christians run into is that our faith is flat. It sounds like Christianity. It bears a resemblance to Christianity. But there is no depth. Something is missing.

We tend to resemble the churches we attend, and in the last couple of decades, there has been movement in many churches to become one-dimensional. They emphasize one primary category while de-emphasizing others. The church and its members define themselves and express their faith in Jesus in a one-dimensional fashion.

God is a three-dimensional God. He is the Father, Son, and Holy Spirit. We are made in His image. We are three-dimensional people. We are soul, mind, and body. A relationship between a three-dimensional God and three-dimensional people should be experienced in a three-dimensional fashion.

So, what we need are three-dimensional churches that love

God, love people, and love the mission of Jesus. We need churches that do things like pray for One because praying for One opens up a community of believers to the fullness of discipleship.

It is similar to the age-old argument that churches have had for years. "Are we going to be a church that disciples or a church that evangelizes?" YES!

You cannot be one without being the other. Discipleship and evangelism always go hand-in-hand. It is impossible to separate the two. If people are growing in their love for God and love for people, then they will reproduce spiritually. Separating discipleship from evangelism is insane, but what is even crazier is the tendency to pit them against each other like they are in competition with one another.

Church leaders struggle with how to allocate limited resources and feel forced to choose between inward- and outward-focused programs. Tension arises between meeting needs within the body and reaching out into the community. Praying for One breaks this tension by keeping our aim always on the functional purpose of the Church. There is no distinction between outreach and in-reach because everything is done for the purpose of seeing more people in the Kingdom of Heaven.

Do we provide pastoral care? Yes, because it helps get more people into the Kingdom of Heaven. Do we do children's programs? Yes, because they help get more people into the Kingdom of Heaven. Do we have small groups, take mission trips, and have killer weekend worship services? Yes, because they help get more people into the Kingdom of Heaven.

In recent years certain buzzwords have emerged to describe three primary types of churches. There are attractional, relational, and missional churches. Each type of church will tell you that their methodology is the right way of doing things and can point out the shortcomings of the others. The problem is that they are all one-dimensional and lacking what the others offer. All three models have value, but their true worth can only be experienced when they are expressed in concert with one another.

connecting people to God

Attractional churches place their focus on connecting people to God. The weekend worship services are often the defining element of the church as people are invited to come and see how great God is. The love of Jesus is experienced through presentation that is well prepared, intentional, engaging, entertaining, compelling, culturally relevant, and full of excellence. High emphasis is placed on members inviting people to church.

Attractional churches pay close attention to what people will experience when they attend a worship service. Buildings are designed to be inviting, comfortable, clean, and easy to navigate. Greeters are often stationed in the parking lot to create a welcoming feeling. Children's ministries are presented as safe, fun, and appealing. The church is sensitive to guests and makes great efforts to attract, welcome, and retain new people.

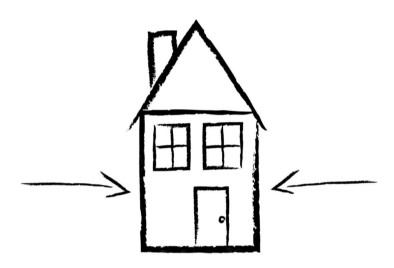

connecting people to people

Relational churches place their focus on connecting people to people. Community is the defining element of the church as people are encouraged to express the love of God through relational experiences. Small groups are key.

These churches vary in size from individual house churches to huge mega churches, but conceptually they share the same driving force. Everything revolves around relational connectivity. Emphasis is placed on mentoring, personal discipleship, discussion, and intimacy. The church is often decentralized, as the focus is less on a church building and more on home-based.

A great deal of effort is placed into the development and promotion of a dynamic network of groups that collectively represent the mission of the church. People are often invited into a small group experience before they ever attend a larger worship gathering. Relational churches recognize that the first and greatest human problem is loneliness, and they make attacking loneliness their number one priority.

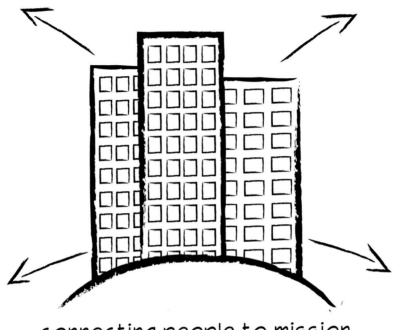

connecting people to mission

Missional churches place their focus on connecting people to mission. Active expressions of faith in Jesus are what define the church, and people are encouraged to live out their faith in the real world. Community service, generosity, and meeting physical needs are primary ways that the gospel is shared with others.

Missional churches are less "come and see" and more "go and do" in their methodology. Emphasis is moved away from anything deemed inward-focused and placed on sending Christians out. It is not uncommon for missional churches to cancel weekend services on occasion to utilize that time to be involved in some form of community action. Members see themselves as an integral part of the mission of the church because participation in the church is centered around active expressions of faith.

Each of these dimensions holds extreme value, but if one is highlighted disproportionately over the others, problems will ensue.

Attractional churches often become more about the show than the gospel. When the emphasis is all on attracting people, the desire not to offend can strip the gospel of power. Pride enters through the competitive nature of comparing numbers. There can be a "my church is better than your church because we have more people in our services" mentality. A revolving door effect begins as people are drawn in for a period of time and then exit because they desire more. The show is not sufficient. People in attractional churches often feel disconnected from others and struggle to find outlets to appropriately express their faith in Jesus.

Relational churches often struggle with legalism, cliquishness, and low evangelistic energy. When the emphasis is all on connecting relationally with other Christians, the "holy huddle" effect takes hold. The church has a tendency to turn inward, latch on to one another, and guard against evil outside influences. Pride enters through comparing relative holiness. There can be a "my church is better than your church because we have more spiritual depth" mentality. People in relational churches can struggle to see the connection between their faith experience and the overall mission of Christ to seek and save the lost.

Missional churches often become so action-oriented that they forget the crucial nature of words and worship. The gospel must be preached with words. How can people hear if the gospel is not preached? God is also revealed through the worship of His people. Allowing people who are apart from Christ to experience authentic worship is one of the best ways to demonstrate the reality of a God who loves them. When the emphasis is all on going and doing, one of the best evangelistic tools the church has to offer is neglected as the corporate worship gathering is relegated to a second- or third-tier experience. Things as simple as cancelling a Sunday morning worship service to go and serve the community can communicate to the church that worshiping together in the classic sense does not hold much value. Pride enters through becoming works-based instead of faith-based. There can be a "my church is better than your church because we do more for the community" mentality. People in missional churches can lose sight of the awesomeness of communal worship and the critical component of preaching the gospel with words.

The Body of Christ is attractional, relational, and missional. It is all three and should never be experienced without the depth that the three-in-one provide. A one-dimensional church is out of balance and off kilter. It doesn't take long for it to start missing the mark. The functional aim will move away from more people in the Kingdom of Heaven and become about something else. A minor deviation in aim, experienced over time, will cause the Church to become utterly ineffective in seeking and saving the lost.

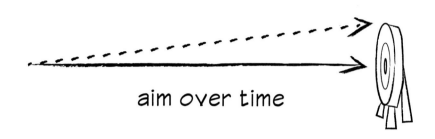

aim over time

The more time that passes, the greater the chance of missing the mark.

The tension between the three dimensions is critical to keep the Church on point. Praying for One creates a church environment that is attractional, relational, and missional. When the primary prayer on every member's lips is for God to give them each One person to share His love with, there is an explosion of depth and fruitfulness.

The aim of the Church is correct because everyone wants the same thing…more people in the Kingdom of Heaven. There is no time or energy for silly arguments about minor doctrines. There is no time or energy for complaining about not being fed. There is no time or energy for dividing over worship styles, building décor, small group methodology, personal offenses, and the like.

When the thrust of the Church is praying for One, it is propelled into exponential multiplication. The force of this movement is so great that everyone hangs on for the ride of their lives. Nobody wants to stop praying for One because life finally makes sense when lived through the mission of Jesus. Since nobody is willing to stop praying for One, the Church must stay on point through being three-dimensional.

Attractional, relational, and missional methodology hold

extreme value when they work in concert with one another. They actually feed into one another and create a cyclical pattern of dynamic growth. These three dimensions are pulled right out of the Great Commandment (to love God and people) and the Great Commission (to make disciples). Praying for One is a thread running through them that binds them together. A church that prays for One can experience the tremendous joy and confidence that comes from being three-dimensional.

The issue surrounding being three-dimensional is not one of balance but one of value. Every church, and every person for that matter, is going to be drawn more heavily to one of the three. They will connect with one more than the others and will highlight that particular dimension. Churches, just like people, have different personalities, and that is part of the beauty of the local church. Praying for One holds the Church accountable to the fullness of discipleship by placing equal value on each dimension. When everyone is praying for One, nobody is willing to settle for less than God's best. We become mature and complete, not lacking anything needed for effective ministry.

Each church will experience varying degrees of effectiveness in each of the three dimensions based on the personality, passions, and resources available to that local congregation. For instance, a church with an amazing building in an excellent location might be more attractional than a church plant meeting in an elementary school buried deep within a neighborhood. It makes sense for each church to emphasize what they are best equipped to do, but at the same time, the depth of all three dimensions must be present.

So, should churches be attractional? Absolutely! Jesus is attractive. The gospel is attractive. Eternal life is attractive. Churches that intentionally sabotage the attractiveness of the gospel would serve Christ's Kingdom better by shutting their doors and never claiming to be a church again. Attractional methodology does not need to be the primary emphasis of every church, but every church should value it. Whatever resources are available should be utilized with excellence. Excellence is not a comparison game because excellence is doing your best with what you have to work with. When you pray for One, there is a desire to invite people to experience the power of God's presence.

Should churches be relational? Of course! Relational connectivity is a crucial component of praying for One. The personal nature of praying for One will drive people into more intimate community. When you pray for One, God increases your relational desires. There is a compulsion to connect with people because every person could be your One. Christ-centered, relational connectivity sends an incredible message to the world. It says, "Look. This is different. Loneliness is not accepted here. We love one another, and you are loved too."

Should churches be missional? Indeed! Authentic faith demands action. Praying for One is certainly not passive. When you pray for One, tangible expressions of faith are required. You go and do so that you can invite people to come and see. God uses His Church in action to put His love on display. It is similar to the miracles. Why did Jesus perform miracles? Scholars and theologians list many reasons, but one of the most compelling is that Jesus is compassionate. His compassionate love moved Him to act. When we pray for One, we tap into the compassionate love of Jesus, and we must release that love into the world around us.

So, what do we conclude? The Church (collectively – all Christians everywhere, locally – groups of Christ followers worshiping together under the authority of a local church, and individually – the personal responsibility to participate in the Great Commandment and Great Commission) must be attractional, relational, and missional. Different elements may be emphasized at times based on a variety of factors, but all must be valued and expressed.

When Christians are flat, they are ineffective. Praying for One provides the necessary depth and preparedness for every good work. Church in 3D is exactly what we need to be. Attractional, relational, and missional methodology working together allow the Church to go all in on building Christ's Kingdom. Pray for One, and you will become attractional, relational, missional, and, most importantly, efficiently effective.

WHY NOT DOUBLE?

chapter seven

WHY NOT DOUBLE?

Throughout history there have been many times when the Church experienced the explosiveness of exponential growth. On day one at Pentecost, the Lord added 3,000 people to their number. Can you imagine the logistical nightmares that came out of that kind of instant growth?

How did the early Church leaders manage the growth and navigate through the messiness that it surely brought?

Initially they did not manage it, and that was a key ingredient to the rapid spread of the gospel. Instead of trying to control the growth, they simply experienced the growth. There were not a lot of thoughts about creating some kind of sustainable infrastructure to maintain individual sets of localized congregations over long periods of time. The focus was on more people in the Kingdom of Heaven, and they fully expected Jesus to return at any given moment.

Time, political pressure, greed, fear, and fatigue have many times knocked the Church off kilter and adjusted the overall aim. God is always faithful to bring the winds of inspiration and revival. When His Body begins to lag in His mission, God shakes things up a bit.

The Holy Spirit stirs within the hearts of believers and they become completely unsatisfied with anything less than God's best. They begin to question. They start to pray expectantly. They visualize lost people being saved. They move beyond the trappings of worldly success and will settle for nothing short of eternal significance.

Then God unleashes His Church for the harvest.

The harvest is plentiful.

Praying for One triggers a release of evangelistic energy that demands exponential growth. One will become two. Two will become four. Four will become eight. As each new person catches the vision to pray for One, he or she is swept up in the momentum of fantastic Kingdom expansion. Suddenly life is no longer about building personal kingdoms because the compulsion to build Christ's Kingdom is dominant.

That is when it starts to get a little scary.

The control freaks among us will begin to panic because they struggle with figuring out how to contain the growth. The less evangelistically-motivated will panic because of feelings of insignificance. The life-long consumers of God begin to panic because they are confronted with the truth that church is not all about them.

People will get concerned that the church is too focused on lost people. Please consider the utter asinine nature of that sentiment. How could Christ's Church ever be too focused on His expressed mission to seek and save the lost?

You can hear the complaints now, can't you?

"What about our needs?"

"What about our children?"

"How are we going to get spiritually fed?"

"We don't want to be a mile wide and an inch deep."

The discomfort will grow as precious resources are utilized more for seeking and saving the lost and less for Christian baby-sitting. Some will not be able to handle it. They have been told for so long that church was about them that the change in aim will be beyond comprehension.

This is precisely why praying for One is so crucial. When the entire church prays for One, everyone gets on board. God makes a directional shift in every heart and mobilizes His Body for purposeful action.

Does it work?

Yes! I have seen it. I am experiencing it.

My church, Manchester Christian Church, prays for One. Our story is valid in demonstrating the effectiveness of praying for One. I will use numbers to help tell this story because numbers are helpful in painting the picture of how God can use a church that prays for One.

The first sermon I preached at Manchester Christian Church was about praying for One. I shared the concept, simplicity, and potential outcome of praying for One. The people connected to the message and were eager to begin praying daily for One.

I told them if we all prayed for One that our church would double in two years. In retrospect that seems like kind of a crazy thing to say on my first Sunday as the Senior Pastor, but I believed it with all my heart.

I am sure that there were some who thought things like: "Oh, isn't that cute? He thinks that our church will double. Doesn't he know that we are already one of the biggest churches in New Hampshire? Doesn't he know that New Hampshire is the least religious state in our country? Doesn't he know that evangelistic work in New Hampshire is like plowing concrete? Doesn't he know that New Englanders are not trusting of outsiders? Doesn't he know that New Englanders are fiercely independent? Doesn't he know that this doubling he speaks of is irrational and impossible? Doesn't he know that he is replacing an amazing Senior Pastor who served here for 30 years? Doesn't he know that studies show that we will most likely experience a 20-40% decrease over the next two years as he begins his ministry here?"

The answer is "yes." Yes, I am cute, and yes, I did know all of those things. I just did not care!

There is a time and place for practical realities to be considered, but praying for One changes reality. I know what God wants to do and what He can do. When people connect to the heart of God through praying for One, growth is the inevitable outcome. The prayer is so compelling because it can be prayed more boldly than any other prayer. Asking God for One person to share His love with is the greatest no brainer in the history of prayer. God's answer is "yes."

On that first Sunday in September, a church committed to pray for One. We accepted the challenge, we started praying right there in the service, and we have not stopped since. Praying for One is mentioned every Sunday and in every email I send our church. When people want to know what we do at Manchester Christian Church, everyone knows that the answer is that we pray for One.

There is synergy, movement, and momentum behind this collective prayer. "Pray for One" has entered our vernacular. People talk openly about their Ones. Everyone has a "pray for One" story. People bring guests and walk around introducing them as their "One." I have even had somebody come up to me on their first Sunday at the church and excitedly proclaim, "I am a One."

Praying for One is FUN! We are having the time of our lives. Church is exciting. People are being saved. Lives are being transformed. The Holy Spirit is working with mighty power. Worship is alive. Joy is the norm. Nobody is the least bit interested in ceasing to pray for One.

But does it work?

Absolutely!

In the first four years of praying for One as a church our weekly attendance almost tripled, the number of campuses tripled, and we baptized over 1,500 people.

Is this kind of growth sustainable? I have no idea, but sustainability is not my primary concern. People are being saved!

When I write that people are being saved, I mean that total life transformation is happening. They are not just becoming church attenders. They are praying for One and are fully-functioning disciples of Jesus who love God, love people, and reproduce spiritually.

Some will argue, "Well, how can you know that? There has not been enough time to determine if true Christian fruit is being exhibited."

I say, "That is a bunch of baloney!"

Where did Christians come up with the ridiculous notion that maturity in Christ can happen only over extended periods of time? Chew on that for a little bit. The Devil has gained a tremendous foothold in our churches by convincing us that only slow growth is good growth. That is totally false. Trust me, from someone who is experiencing it, rapid growth is incredible.

I am not just referring to the rapid growth in numbers. I also mean the rapid growth of Christ in people. We have worked hard to remove the barriers of time from disciple-making by moving from a linear process to an organic experience. Pray for One is a message for everyone. It holds meaning for the thoroughly un-churched and reveals to them what following Christ will entail. It also holds tremendous depth for someone who has been walking with Christ for decades by constantly reminding them of the functional purpose driving their pursuit of Jesus.

The floodgates for rapid growth are thrown open when people are immediately released to participate in building God's Kingdom.

Last year I met a man named Mike. Mike lives near a park downtown where a ministry from our church serves breakfast to homeless and low-income people every Saturday and Sunday. One Sunday, Mike went to the park and had breakfast. While he was there, someone engaged him with the gospel, and Mike surrendered his life to Christ.

After breakfast, he caught a ride to church, and that is when we met. Mike came into our church excited about his new relationship with Jesus. I will never forget meeting him because of the genuine wonder in his eyes. Someone introduced Mike to me, and he said, "Oh, good. You're the Pastor. I was hoping to talk to you because I just had breakfast in the park, and this person told me about Jesus and showed me some things in the Bible. I prayed with them and asked Jesus to be my Lord and Savior. So since I did that, what am I supposed to do now?"

I simply told Mike to pray for One. I told him to ask God to give him One person every day to share the love of Jesus with and then to pay attention to the opportunities that would be before him. Mike said, "I can do that!"

One week later, Mike came bounding into church after breakfast in the park, and he came over to give me an update on his relationship with Jesus. He said, "Ok, you know that praying for One thing you told me to do? Well, I've been doing that, and I woke up this morning and thought, you know what? Those people who shared Jesus with me were probably praying for One, and they go to the park to serve breakfast every Saturday and Sunday, so I'll go to the park and do what they do. So, I got out of bed and went down to the park to volunteer. They put me right to work, and I had my first Sunday as a volunteer in the Do You Know Him? Ministry. So, what do I do now?"

I told Mike to keep praying for One, and he said, "Can do, Pastor Bo!" and he marched off.

The very next Sunday, Mike showed up at church even more excited than he had been the previous two weeks. He could barely contain himself as he waited in line to speak with me. I could see him behind a couple of people bouncing up and down with a huge smile on his face. When he finally got to talk to me, he could hardly contain himself.

Mike said, "So, I've been doing that pray for One thing like you told me, and this morning I went to the park to serve in my volunteer position with the Do You Know Him? Ministry. I met this lady who didn't know Jesus, so I sat down with her and told her what the people told me two weeks ago. I showed her what they showed me in the Bible, and then she prayed to give her life to Christ. So I got my first One today. What do I do next?"

Can you guess what I told him? That's right. I simply said, "Pray for another One." And that's exactly what Mike is doing.

Not long after that, Mike and I baptized his wife together. Every time I see Mike, he has a testimony to share. Recently he has been delivered from alcoholism. To date, Mike is four months sober. He loves telling people that he used to drink and how Jesus is changing his life. Mike shares God's love with me and with everyone he meets. He is a Praying for One machine.

God uses people like Mike. Mike is the type of guy that the world generally places little value in. He would probably be the guy that would get picked last for kickball in elementary school. He wouldn't be described as smart, wealthy, talented, handsome, and so on. But that is not what God is looking for. Mike has the best characteristic of all…he is available.

It was two weeks from the time Mike was saved until he led his first One to Christ. Two weeks! How long has it been for you?

I am so glad that we were able to give Mike clear direction on what to do next. More people are in the Kingdom of Heaven because Jesus captivated Mike's heart. We did not tell Mike to get off alcohol, clean up his language, join a Bible study group, take a series of classes, and so on. We just told Mike to pray for One. That's what he is doing, but guess what? On his own, Mike has decided to get off alcohol, clean up his language, join a Bible study group, and take classes. He wants to do all those things so that he is more effective at sharing God's love with each and every One God puts in his path.

I cannot tell the story of what God is doing in Manchester Christian Church without sharing stories like Mike's. We have tons of them because the exponential growth we are experiencing is all driven by praying for One. Our church doubled in size in two years because we pray for One.

Churches grow for lots of reasons. Sometimes the growth comes from the completion of a building project, the introduction of a dynamic new ministry, the failing of another church, and so on. Often leaders cannot articulate why their church is growing.

We know why Manchester Christian Church is growing... we pray for One, but we also make a way for One.

I see no valid reason to inhibit a church's growth. Why not pray, plan, and prepare to double? If everyone in your church is praying for One, shouldn't you expect exponential growth?

There are practical realities to consider. The most obvious and most often neglected issue regarding church growth is the number of available seats. Here's the deal. People (churched or un-churched) want to attend worship services on Sundays between 9:00 and 11:00 a.m. I am not saying that there is no value in alternate worship times (Saturday, etc.), but the practical reality is that people are most likely to attend church between 9:00 and 11:00 a.m. on Sunday mornings. Simple logic dictates that if you are going to pray for One and double every couple of years, then you are going to need twice as many seats.

It's simple and obvious, but I missed it in the past. Before becoming the Senior Pastor at Manchester Christian Church, I was a failed church planter. People hate the word "fail" in the context of church, but the fact of the matter is that our church plant failed. We started a church from scratch with the intention of growing a dynamic body of Christ-followers that would impact the community for generations to come.

93

That church plant no longer exists though, so by definition it failed. We failed. Don't get me wrong. We know that God did many wonderful things through the church plant. There were many people who were saved, and life change occurred. I don't want to diminish that, but by the same token, I'm not comfortable ignoring how my leadership flaws and other factors stopped the church from growing and led to its ultimate demise.

Like most church planters, I had a big vision. We did some prelaunch meetings, and God drew a group of people together that was inspired to change a region. The church began in an elementary school and had 150 people attending from almost day one. Within two months of starting the church, God laid the concept of Pray for One on my heart. I began to share it passionately with the church, and the people eagerly jumped at the opportunity to be active participants in building God's Kingdom.

Everyone was praying for One, and sure enough, we began to grow. I had studied and prepared for church planting. I knew the statistics about how large a plant could grow in different types of facilities. I knew that churches meeting in elementary schools rarely grew above 200 members, and the average attendance was much, much lower. The only facility available to us was an elementary school, and sure enough, we reached a point of repulsion quickly. We would have a Sunday with 185 in attendance, then drop to 160 the following Sunday, and then slowly creep back up to 185 to 200 before contracting again.

I understood the practical reality of our situation, but I assumed that we would be different. For some crazy reason, I thought that our church plant would be the exception to the rule, so we just pressed forward thinking that we could double to 400 people in that elementary school. Oops! The validity of the Praying for One message remained, but our people stopped actually doing it. They knew that praying for One could work because God brought people into their lives to share His love with, but practically speaking, there was no room in our church for any more Ones.

The people would nod and smile in agreement as each Sunday I reminded everyone to pray for One, but it did not take long for them to realize subconsciously that praying for One without making a way for One is essentially pointless. Since this was the primary messaging and methodology for our church, I basically lost all leadership credibility. The people still liked me. They liked the church. But like does not translate into personal buy in.

After suffering several facility let downs over a few years, we decided that it was time to stop playing pretend and deal with reality. Praying for One cannot work without having room for One.

Now for the cynically minded reader who thinks seats do not matter and that large churches are not the answer, I would like for you to consider the Parable of the Talents found in Matthew 25:14-30.

"Again, it will be like a man going on a journey, who called his servants and entrusted his property to them. To one he gave five talents of money, to another two talents, and to another one talent, each according to his ability. Then he went on his journey. The man who had received the five talents went at once and put his money to work and gained five more. So also, the one with the two talents gained two more. But the man who had received the one talent went off, dug a hole in the ground and hid his master's money.

"After a long time the master of those servants returned and settled accounts with them. The man who had received the five talents brought the other five. 'Master,' he said, 'you entrusted me with five talents. See, I have gained five more.'

"His master replied, 'Well done, good and faithful servant! You have been faithful with a few things; I will put you in charge of many things. Come and share your master's happiness!'

"The man with the two talents also came. 'Master,' he said, 'you entrusted me with two talents; see, I have gained two more.'

"His master replied, 'Well done, good and faithful servant! You have been faithful with a few things; I will put you in charge of many things. Come and share your master's happiness!'

"Then the man who had received the one talent came. 'Master,' he said, 'I knew that you are a hard man, harvesting where you have not sown and gathering where you have not scattered seed. So I was afraid and went out and hid your talent in the ground. See, here is what belongs to you.'

"His master replied, 'You wicked, lazy servant! So you knew that I harvest where I have not sown and gather where I have not scattered seed? Well then, you should have put my money on deposit with the bankers, so that when I returned I would have received it back with interest.

"'Take the talent from him and give it to the one who has the ten talents. For everyone who has will be given more, and he will have an abundance. Whoever does not have, even what he has will be taken from him. And throw that worthless servant outside, into the darkness, where there will be weeping and gnashing of teeth.'"

It is the responsibility of every local church to reach as many people as possible. They must leverage every resource at their disposal for the purpose of seeing more people in the Kingdom of Heaven. Sometimes churches that want to appear deep, bury their talents. Can you imagine standing before Jesus at judgment and giving an account for a church that refused to build the Kingdom?

What would you say? Would it be something like this?

"Hey, Jesus. We are really excited to see you here. We took the people you entrusted us with, and we got them really deep into your Word. Now we didn't actually reach any new people, but the ones we started with are a lot better at worship, Bible study, long flowing prayers, and their sin management skills are impeccable. So, how did we do?"

Hmm...how did we do?

So many churches play it safe. They batten down the hatches and try to hold on in survival mode. Instead of risking it all to see more people in the Kingdom of Heaven, they bury their talents deep because they are afraid. The only things we ought to be burying are dead things. Churches that bury their talents are dead.

But hey! God is in the resurrection business, right?

Praying for One and making a way for One can resurrect any church.

These lessons on dealing with practical realities were not lost on me. When I became the Senior Pastor at Manchester Christian Church, I carried with me the knowledge of how ignoring the need for something as simple as more seats can totally kill a church's momentum. When 1,200 people committed to pray for One, I knew that we needed find a way to make room for 2,400 people.

When there were 2,400 people praying for One, we knew that we needed to make a way for there to be seats for 4,800 people.

We committed our best minds to this problem of always having enough seats to continue praying for One and landed on a multi-site strategy. Being one church in multiple locations allows for an unlimited amount of seats. Of course there is cost involved in this, but one of the best parts about praying for One is that the people are all responsible.

When I needed to stand up in front of Manchester Christian Church to raise money for more seats, it was easy. I simply told the church that we were doubling and that it was all their fault. I reminded them that the growth was the result of praying for One and that we had no intention of not praying for One, so we better pull together and make a way for One. They opened their hearts and their wallets, and in one year we went from one site to three so that there could be enough seats for us to continue praying for One.

So, why not double? Honestly, there are lots of reasons not to double. Sometimes circumstances are just out of our control. I don't know what tomorrow holds. A fire, a scandal, a split, or just plain old-fashioned poor leadership could wipe out Manchester Christian Church.

All I know is that I believe with all my heart that if we pray for One and make a way for One, then there will be more people in the Kingdom of Heaven. We should never settle for less, and if Christians would just keep doubling, the whole world could be reached with the love of Jesus!

RISKY BUSINESS

chapter eight

RISKY BUSINESS

Praying for One is not safe. It is not cheap. It is not all sunshine, rainbows, and lollipops.

Praying for One is risky. It is not for the faint of heart. Those content with the status quo need not apply.

Praying for One will destroy the mental checklist of all the things that you will not do for God that you carry close to your heart for personal protection. It will lead you to throw caution to the wind. You will go places no self-righteous Christian would ever go. You will have conversations that would cause the easily offended to blush with indignant shame. You will touch people that most churches at best would simply just ignore or at worst would point the bony finger of judgment at and shout, "Unclean!"

Praying for One moves you to the lunatic fringe. It takes you out of the realm of cultural Christianity and moves you into the divine flow of Holy Spirit action. Simply put, when you pray for One, it is going to get crazy.

Crazy is good. Following Jesus is supposed to be crazy. It should be dangerous. It ought to be wild and adventurous. Christianity is an out-of-this-world experience. Christ followers are strangers and aliens on this earth. This place is not our home. We serve as ambassadors for a better home...a heavenly home. That mission gets lost when we get comfortable in this time and place.

Praying for One draws attention Heavenward. It lifts the believer out of the emptiness of Christian clichés and into raging depths of Christ's love. Christians are notorious for spouting clever little sayings designed to placate and console. We say things like, "The safest place in the world to be is at the center of God's will." Hmm...safe? I don't think so. It is not safe at all.

Safe? No. Good? Yes.

There is no promise of personal protection in following Jesus. That thought alone is enough to rock some to their theological core. Many hold a foundational belief that God would never allow anything "bad" to happen to them. They may not verbalize it, but the ideology is there. This type of thinking blocks the effectiveness of praying for One.

When the primary worldview is one of self-preservation, praying for One is rendered essentially impotent. We need to understand right up front that seeking and saving the lost is dangerous work. Simple logic ought to confirm this line of thinking.

Christians are Christ followers. That means that we do what Jesus did.

What did Jesus do? He came to this earth and gave His life as a ransom for many. Jesus explicitly told us to take up our crosses and follow Him. He told us that whoever wants to save his life will lose it, but whoever loses his life for Christ's sake will gain eternity.

Why would we ever think that following Jesus would produce different results for us than it did for Him and His first disciples? Are we more favored? Are we better? Has the mission changed?

The mission has not changed and the stakes are still just as high. Is this scary? Absolutely, but I can tell you from experience that it beats the Hell out not living for Jesus. (FYI...there is no need to be offended...Hell was used in the appropriate biblical sense in the previous sentence and not as a curse word...Hell is separation from God, and living for Jesus conquers Hell...you can do the math.)

Yeah, but...

No.

Let's keep our buts to ourselves. I know that we have some really big buts. Sometimes we like our big buts more than we like the truth of Jesus.

I cannot lie; the issue of "buts" is a struggle. What I have found, though, is that praying for One helps me overcome my objections to following Jesus. He counters my big buts with a better hope. I have no need to build a personal kingdom when I am sharing in His eternal Kingdom!

One of my early pray for One encounters put this notion of risk to the test. It was during my church planting days when a man named Steve walked into our Sunday service for the first time. We were meeting in a bar in a soccer stadium at the time, and Steve came in just after the service started and sat alone on the front row. Our little church was extremely tuned in to welcoming guests, so despite his best efforts to go unnoticed, we were all very aware of his presence.

Steve began to cry very soon after finding his seat, and he continued crying through the entire service. After the closing song, we gave him a moment or two to compose himself before we pounced. He was welcomed, introduced around, given information about the church, and loved on in a very sincere fashion.

Steve returned the following Sunday and proceeded to cry through the service a second time. On that day, I had the opportunity to hear a little bit of his story. Steve was recently divorced. He was in financial ruin. Alcohol had a major grip on him.

Steve's world was in utter chaos. The first half of his life had been spent chasing financial gain. He lived by himself in a big house. He drove a sports car he could not afford. He had expensive taste in clothes and jewelry. Image was everything, but he had nothing. Debt was crushing him, and the pressures of life had become unmanageable.

When Steve came to church for the third week in a row, I asked if he would like to have lunch one day. He agreed to meet me two days latter. He also picked up a copy of a book I had written and told me that he would start reading it along with the Bible to help pull him through the week.

We met for lunch on a Tuesday, and I could tell that Steve was still pretty skeptical about the whole church thing. I decided to take a blatantly honest approach with him. I shared my struggles with him. I listened intently to all that he was facing. I pointed him to Jesus. Steve agreed that we should continue the conversation, and he told me that he had started reading my book. I gave him my cell phone number and told him to text or call anytime.

Steve sent me a text message two days later at 9:30 p.m. The text read, "I'm on page 54. Come over."

Now let me tell you...I lead a pretty exciting life. I mean, I like the nightlife...I like to party, but on this particular Thursday night I was in my pajamas and had closed up shop for the night. My wife and kids were snuggled in bed, and I was watching a little television before calling it a night myself.

I had no idea where Steve lived, and I had no intention of going to his house by myself after 10:00 p.m. But before responding to his text message, I prayed for him. After all, I was praying for One, and there was little doubt that Steve was an answer to prayer. As I prayed, I felt the urge to look up page 54 in the book I had written. I flipped open the book and realized that Steve was reading about how we must surrender everything to God and receive Jesus as Lord.

Here is page 54 in its entirety.

We preach freedom and live in bondage. We proclaim life and dwell in death. Christians are tired, angry, and frustrated because we choose to carry burdens we are not meant to hold. The journey is hard enough on its own; we don't need the added weight of baggage.

Jesus wants to strip us of this heavy load so that we can follow Him. If we follow Him, we live. If we live, He is glorified. Put your burden down. You don't really need it. Jesus is sufficient.

One of the things that I love about Jesus is that He always seems to do things in an 'over-the-top' fashion. He always goes above and beyond.

Like, in this case, He doesn't just want us to surrender our burdens to Him. He offers a trade-in.

Jesus promises to give us everything that we need. He says that when we keep in step with the Spirit, then certain things will be produced. It is called fruit. Perhaps you have heard of the fruit of the Spirit. This fruit is love, joy, peace, patience, kindness, goodness, faithfulness, gentleness, and self-control. All of these produce freedom.

So, if we lay our burdens down and follow Jesus, He gives us a new reality. He takes our junk and replaces it with life. We are no longer burdened but free.

Think about it.

(I'm Going to Light Myself on Fire,
Bo Chancey, p. 54)

As soon as I read that, I knew that I had to go to Steve's house. He was ready to surrender his life to Christ, and he wanted me to share in that most sacred moment. I sent Steve a text message asking where he lived. It turned out that he only lived about two miles away from me. I let him know that I would be over ASAP, and that was when it got risky.

I walked upstairs into the master bedroom and started to put some clothes on. My wife said, "What are you doing?"

I replied, "I'm going over to Steve's house."

She asked, "Who is Steve?"

I said, "You know, the guy I had lunch with on Tuesday."

She said, "No, I do not know that guy. Who is Steve?"

I said, "You know…he's the guy that has come to church the last three weeks, sits on the front row, and cries through the service."

She said, "No, I do not know him. Who is Steve?"

I said, "I told you about him. He's the lonely guy who is recently divorced, addicted to alcohol, facing bankruptcy, and is really depressed."

She said, "Oh…so what makes you think that going to his house alone at 10:00 on a Thursday night is a good idea?"

I said, "He's on page 54."

She said, "What's page 54?"

I said, "It's about surrender. Steve wants to give his life to Christ. He wants me to come over and pray with him."

She asked, "Can't that wait until tomorrow?"

I said, "No! He's ready right now. I have to go."

She said, "You are not going over there alone tonight."

I asked, "Why not?"

She said, "It's too dangerous. You don't know this guy. You don't know anybody who knows this guy. He is depressed, under the influence of alcohol, and is highly unpredictable. You can't go."

Now just to be clear. My wife often serves as the voice of reason in our relationship. I listen to her. God uses her more in my life than any other human. I respect her and the points she made were absolutely valid. Our relationship is filled with mutual trust and respect. Normally I would have totally conceded to her wishes, but this was different. This was a pray for One moment.

I told her, "I have to go."

She said, "I am not okay with you going to his house. If you have to go, call him and see if he will meet you for coffee. That way I know that you are safe and are in a public setting."

Seeing that this was a perfectly reasonable alternative, I agreed to call him to set up a place to meet.

I called Steve and said, "Let's go grab some coffee and talk."

Steve said, "No. I'm already on my fifth beer. Come over because there is something that I need to give to you."

For some crazy reason this made sense to me so I said, "Okay, I'll be there in ten minutes."

I went back into the bedroom and told my wife what Steve had said. The fact that Steve was on beer number five did not comfort her in the least, but she knew that I was going to his house.

She rolled over in bed and said, "Well, I guess if you are going to die, getting shot by a lonely, depressed drunk guy in his house late at night because he is on page 54 of your book is about as good a way to go as any."

I kissed her on the head, and she said, "Send me a text message in an hour or so to let me know if you are not dead."

That final sentence my wife said to me really stuck in my head. The whole way over to Steve's house, I prayed for him, but I also got fixated on how he might kill me. The reality that I did not know this guy and that he was really unstable started to mess with my head. As I prayed, I made a decision that if it was time to die, then I would die for Jesus. I know that seems dramatic, but that was the state of mind I was in when I arrived at Steve's house.

I pulled into Steve's driveway, and he was waiting for me in his garage. I was kind of hoping that maybe we could just stay outside and talk, but he immediately had me follow him inside. We walked into his kitchen, and he popped open another beer. Steve was different than I had seen him on other occasions. He was calm. His words were steady, and his thoughts were clear. The difference in him was a bit unnerving.

We stood at the bar in his kitchen, and he thanked me for coming over. He said that he wanted to surrender his life to Christ and that he had something to give me. I asked him if he wanted to pray together, and he said, "Yes." We prayed, and Steve asked Jesus to be his Lord and Savior.

When we finished praying, Steve told me why page 54 had such an impact on him. He said that he had spent his entire adult life trying to be successful through the accumulation of stuff. Possessions and status symbols were his gods. He told me that he collected expensive watches and that there was one watch in particular that was his favorite. He said that it was the first big-ticket item he had ever purchased and that, of all his watches, it was the one that most symbolized his life up to that point. Since he was starting a new life with Christ, he wanted to give me that watch, and he asked if I would pray for him each time I put it on.

I was nervous about accepting such an expensive and meaningful gift, but his eyes expressed a sincerity and genuineness that I could not deny. I told him that I would take the watch on two conditions. The first was that, if at any time he wanted it back, I would return it to him with no questions asked. The second was that I would pray for him when I put it on, but he would have to agree to pray for One whenever he put his watch on. Steve agreed to both conditions and then told me to follow him into the closet in his master bedroom where he kept his safe.

As we walked through his bedroom, I spotted a shotgun sticking out from behind his bed. The sight of that gun sent a surge of panic through me as I remembered my wife's comments about dying, and I thought about a scene from a movie I had just seen.

I had recently watched a movie where a couple of thieves had double-crossed each other. In the final scene, one thief had the other at gunpoint and forced him to open a floor safe where the stolen money was stashed. With one last plot twist, the guy at gunpoint reached into the safe, pulled out a hidden gun, and shot the other thief.

As we moved through Steve's bathroom and into his closet, I became certain that I was about to die. I just knew that, as he bent down to open the safe, he would pull a gun out and shoot me. My heart was racing. I had totally psyched myself out. I had forgotten all about the watch, so when he took it out and turned to hand it to me, I was on my heels backing up and out of the closet. He looked at me kind of strangely as my arms were raised near my chest in a symbolic gesture of surrender. Steve extended the watch to me and said, "Here…try it on."

The fact that he was holding a watch and not a gun brought tremendous relief. I placed the watch on my wrist as Steve told me all about why the watch was so valuable to him. This was a huge moment for him, but it was also a major turning point for me. The risk involved in praying for One had become a reality.

Steve and I went into his living room and sat down on his couches to continue our chat. My wife sent me a text message to see if I was still alive. While I was responding to her, Steve realized how late it was and that I was married. He immediately started apologizing for getting me out of my house so late at night, and he asked if my wife was angry with me.

I said, "No, she is not angry. She is worried and scared."

Steve got a really confused look on his face as he tried to figure out why my wife would be worried. I saw him trying to mentally connect the dots, and then it clicked. Steve said, "Oh... tell her I'm not gay!"

I said, "Buddy, that's the least of her worries."

He looked confused again.

When I told him that she was afraid that he was going to kill me, he started to laugh. I chuckled too but confessed that I had been pretty rattled by the whole encounter. I told him that, when I saw the shotgun sticking out from behind his bed, I was convinced I was about to be shot.

Steve got a kick out of that then proceeded to tell me that he had only fired that shotgun once inside his house. He took me into the dining room where there was a shotgun blast through the wall. He told me that he had been ready to kill himself but decided not to at the last minute, so he just shot a hole through the wall instead.

I explained to Steve that, with his history of depression, keeping a loaded gun in the house was a bad idea. We prayed together and each asked God to give us One person to share His love with. Then I went home to a relieved wife.

Steve continues to pray for One, and he has shared the love of Jesus with tons of people. I have worn that watch every day for years, and when I look at it, I think about Steve and how praying for One is changing me. I take risks that I wouldn't have before, and life is much more exciting.

Praying for One is going to pull you out of your comfort zone. It will inconvenience you. It will cost you. It will transform you.

You will speak with people you would have never spoken to before. You will touch people you would have otherwise ignored. Jesus will conquer fears, insecurities, and prejudices within you. Excuses will be replaced with expectant prayers for One to share God's love with.

And God's Kingdom will grow.

AND THEN IT GETS WEIRD

chapter nine

AND THEN IT GETS WEIRD

When did normalcy become such a popular goal?

I hear people all the time saying things like, "I just want a normal life, with a normal job, a normal family, and normal relationships."

Honestly, that seems awful. Normal is dependent on a comparison process. The only way to determine if you are normal is by comparing yourself to others. When you do this, you will find envy, coveting, competition, pride, and false views of self.

Jesus commands us to love our neighbors as we love ourselves. It is impossible to love like Jesus when normal is your primary objective. The love of Jesus is an out-of-this-world experience. That is why the Bible refers to Christians as strangers and aliens. Authentic Christ-followers are going to be weird.

Praying for One opens the door for all manner of weirdness. This prayer impacts your baseline understanding of self and positions you to navigate the pitfalls of various self-esteem issues effectively. Some people think too highly of self and are held captive by pride. Others think too lowly of self and are caught in the bondage of perpetual doubt. This is an oversimplification of the psychological issues surrounding the view of self, but the spiritual ramifications of either view result in the same ineffectiveness and purposelessness.

Unfortunately ineffectiveness and purposelessness are both pretty normal. Normal is not good.

It is impossible to obey Christ's command to love your neighbor as yourself when you do not posses a godly view of self. Praying for One connects you to the heartbeat of God and is a constant reminder that you are One. You were lost. You were separated from God. But God pursued you, saved you, and called you to participate in His mission. You have been delivered from meaningless existence into purposeful living.

With this knowledge at the forefront of your mind, you will be compelled to take action. Normal will never satisfy. You will crave weirdness. And that's when it gets really weird.

God will answer your prayers for One in the craziest ways. Your One will appear at the oddest times, in the strangest places, in the most bizarre circumstances. The supernatural cannot be explained away nor should it. Praying for One will open you up to experience the supernatural love of God flowing through you to others. There will be no doubt that God is working because no human could conceive and contrive what unfolds.

Over the last several years, I have heard many Praying for One stories. Some were touching. Some were gut-wrenching. Some were funny. Some were exciting. Each story is unique, but a common denominator in all of them is that they are weird.

Salvation is the best kind of miracle. When you pray for One, people are saved. Praying for One opens up the door for miracles. Miracles, by definition, are weird.

When I first started praying for One, I just assumed that God would answer my prayer in a normal fashion. My thoughts on evangelism were generally focused on specific attempts to take someone through a gospel presentation of some sort with an invitation to receive Christ at the end. I thought that I would pray for One and maybe invite a neighbor to church at some point, and the rest would just kind of take care of itself.

I was not prepared for the messiness of praying for One. I did not anticipate how inconvenient praying for One could be. I never considered how much time, money, and energy praying for One would cost me. And most of all, I totally underestimated the weirdness factor.

And Then You Get Puked On

One time, I met a guy at the gym named James. We were both rounding a corner in the men's locker room from different directions and almost ran into each other. He was covering his mouth with his hand and looked panicked. When I asked if he was okay, he shook his head no and then proceeded to vomit on me.

We bonded over the fact that he threw up on me, and from then on we talked whenever we saw each other at the gym. A couple of months later, I got to baptize James. It is hard to imagine that getting thrown up all over is a direct answer to prayer, but when you pray for One, it gets weird.

James started praying for One, and God introduced him to a young lady named Destiny. James is a recruiter for the Army, and Destiny was a new recruit. James knew that she was his One. He found me at the gym one day and asked me to pray with him

121

for Destiny. James was concerned for Destiny and wanted to do everything in his power to help her know Jesus before she went off to boot camp.

James started helping Destiny train for boot camp, and this gave him the opportunity to introduce her to me at the gym. We invited her to church, and she accepted. Our church adored Destiny, and many people joined James and me in praying for her. It did not take long for Destiny to surrender her life to Christ. She was baptized one summer night at youth group, and everyone cheered like crazy!

Destiny went off to boot camp, but stays in touch with her new church family. She prays for One all the time and God has already used her greatly to share His love with others. She sent me this story about how God has answered her prayers for One.

When I shipped to basic training in the Army, I knew within ten minutes of being there that the experience was going to be a great test of my patience and faith. I have never had much patience, nor have I ever been very good at being nice to those who irritate me or those who I just don't like. I am also very quick to not like people, so you can imagine how quickly I got angry in a room full of 60 females from all different backgrounds from all over the United States.

I knew that I needed to keep my cool and not be rude to people. I decided to try to be kind to everyone, so I started praying hard. There was one female in particular who was loud, cocky, and rude, and she instantly got on my nerves. On just our second night there, she started making fun of me and acted like she owned the barracks. She was bossing everyone around. I don't know if it was the stress of the new environment, the lack of sleep, anger, or a combination of all three, but I lost my temper and went off on her. She didn't hesitate to come right back at me, and we ended up fighting.

We both received negative reports and extra duty assignments after a long lecture from the drill sergeants. I knew this type of behavior was ungodly, so I prayed for patience and help from God to make it in this new environment. I prayed for the people who were rude, obnoxious, or didn't help out in the barracks. I also continued to pray for One knowing that I could participate in God's mission even from boot camp.

All the females got split up and sent to six different companies, so I was hoping that I would be separated from the girl I had fought with. When I arrived at my training battalion, our drill sergeants had us fill out questionnaires about ourselves. They wanted to learn about our personalities and backgrounds. From behind me, I heard this one loud and obnoxious voice complaining about how dumb the questionnaire was. I turned around and saw that it was the girl I had fought with. The entire platoon got punished because of her mouth.

Not only was she in my company, she was also in my platoon. This meant that we would be together for every second of every day for the next ten weeks. Within the first few days, my hatred for her grew exponentially, but I continued to pray for her and for One.

Within the platoon, each of us was assigned a permanent battle buddy. We were not allowed to go anywhere without our battle buddies, and we were supposed to help them whenever they needed it. Teamwork with your battle buddy is essential. If you do not work well together, the drill sergeant will force you to do tons of pushups. You are

123

also bunk and locker mates with your battle buddy, so it is pretty important that you like the person.

When our drill sergeants assigned the battle buddies, they took into consideration our personality questionnaires and tried to match us accordingly. I found myself praying not to be placed with the girl I had fought with, but while the list was being read, I asked God to put me with whomever He wanted.

You can learn a lot from your battle buddy as the two of you grow together during basic training. I really wanted to be with someone who I would enjoy getting to know. Initially, I was partnered with a really quiet girl who I did not know at all. She didn't talk much but was very neat and organized. I was very excited that my battle buddy was going to be pretty low maintenance.

In the second week of basic training, however, my battle buddy was injured and taken out of the Army. I had been praying for One every night, but I hadn't found my One yet, or so I thought. I went a few days without a battle buddy, which I liked at first, but without an assigned buddy you don't really get the opportunity to get close to anyone.

Later that week, I was one of the few people in the barracks cleaning and using my personal time when I heard someone crying in the bathroom. I went in to try to talk to whomever it was and make sure she was okay. It turned out to be the girl I hated so much. I almost just turned around and walked away, but I knew the right thing to do would be to try to comfort her.

We talked for a while, and she opened up to me about how she was so lost and that the Army was her last resort. Her family had abandoned her, and she had nothing and no one. She was completely alone, and everyone hated her because of the way she treated people. The drill sergeants got on her case a lot about it, and she was losing hope in having what it takes to get through basic training in the Army.

I can attest first hand how hard it is to go through basic training without someone by your side. I was struggling too, and I would have been ready to quit if it weren't for the people from church writing me and reminding me that Jesus was by my side. She was talking about quitting, but she didn't know where she would go or what she would do.

I continued to talk with her for quite some time, and even though she told me she wasn't really religious, she agreed to let me pray with her. After that, we started talking and praying every night. I tried to encourage her in her physical training, and my drill sergeants noticed. They decided to make her my permanent battle buddy.

That Sunday I invited her to go to church and Bible study with me. She was hesitant at first but decided to come along. She absolutely loved it and started reading my Bible every night. She asked tons of questions, and we prayed together regularly. Over the next few weeks of training, the two of us got incredibly close, and we saw amazing changes in each other.

There were the normal changes that come with boot camp. We became more disciplined, our vocabulary changed, we were more confident, and we were truly becoming soldiers. But there was more. She became much nicer, and I became more patient. We both became better Christians.

I was blessed to be a part of her baptism at the end of the cycle as she took that next step in giving her life to Jesus.

The following week was family day and graduation. I was not looking forward to either event. I knew no one was coming to see me, and I didn't want to take part in the ceremonies. She noticed I was upset, but we didn't really talk about it.

On family day, my biological dad showed up for the sole purpose of tearing me apart and embarrassing me in front of my platoon and drill sergeants. He completely put me down for everything I had worked so hard for. Fortunately, my drill sergeant took care of him and gave me a little pep talk, but I went back to the barracks instead of going out like everyone else for family day.

About an hour later, my battle buddy showed up at the barracks to comfort me and to get me to go out with her for the day. I haven't seen her since our graduation because we were sent to different places, but not a day has gone by that we have not talked to each other. We call each other every night and pray together. She is my best friend and will always be my battle buddy. I am so grateful that I continued to pray for One because God blessed me with a great friend who helps me love Jesus more.

So to sum this up…I prayed for One, got puked on, and made a friend in James. He gave his life completely to Christ and started praying for One. God answered his prayers for One by putting a young lady in his life that he suddenly felt responsible for. James went beyond the call of duty in reaching out to her and God used him to help Destiny become a Christian. Now Destiny is praying for One and her battle buddy is a Christ-follower who is also praying for One. This all occurred in less than a year!

And Then You Give Blood

I have a friend named Rebecca who loves Jesus and prays

126

for One. She once confided to me that she was a bit frustrated in praying for One, because her lifestyle keeps her from meeting new people. She works from home, goes to school online, and in general is pretty content with limited human interaction. All of those factors can make it a bit difficult to find someone to share God's love with each day.

Rebecca expressed that frustration to God and God answered by directing her to give blood. We were doing a blood drive at our church and Rebecca sensed a direct push from God to participate. Here is Rebecca's story in her own words.

I try to give blood regularly, but unfortunately, I pass out every time. One donation event recently took place at my church, and I went to give. As predicted, I passed out after giving blood. When I came to, I was flipped upside down on a stretcher with a nurse and three phlebotomists standing over me.

After making sure I was okay, the nurse left with instructions to the three phlebotomists to keep me talking so that I wouldn't lose consciousness again. I was feeling very nauseous and knew I could pass out again very easily.

Not knowing me, the trio asked questions about my life. I told them I was married with two daughters and what I did for a living. When I mentioned I went to church there, the trio began asking me questions about my church. That's when I felt that familiar nudge from Jesus to tell them about Him.

My first thought was, "Seriously? Now, Jesus? I may throw up on them!"

But I dove in anyway, willing to take the risk of passing out or throwing up in order to talk to them about Jesus.

The trio went on to tell me each of their own experiences in religion. All three had been exposed to religious rhetoric and doctrine but felt that their religions were missing something.

These three people understood who Jesus was in theory, but their faith was so dead that they couldn't grasp His love for them. Their own religions never talked about Jesus' love or forgiveness. They only taught condemnation and guilt. It was clear to me that none of them had a relationship with the Lord, just a strained relationship with their religion.

Then they asked me questions about my church's beliefs and services. When they compared what I told them with their experiences, they realized that what they believed was so layered in that dogma and tradition that they just assumed every church was the funeral-like experience that they were used to.

They didn't know of Jesus' joy either. It amazed me that these three people could be exposed to lifelong churchy experiences and still not know Jesus!

When they asked about specific teachings that were not biblical, my response was, "If it isn't in the Bible, then we don't teach it. We're nutty and non-denominational... both are a good thing. You should come!"

Then I gave them the service times and locations and told them where they could find me on Sunday. I even said I'd introduce them to our crazy senior pastor! I encouraged them to come and discover the love, forgiveness, and joy of Jesus, our living God, and get out of the dead-zone of religion.

We are often most effective for Jesus in our weakest moments. Rebecca was on the verge of passing out and throwing up when Jesus answered her prayer for One with three. Praying for One opens you up to being used by Jesus at anytime anywhere. Jesus gave His blood for you. What are you willing to give for Him?

And Then You Bring the Devil to Church

God often answers our prayers for One with by giving us the last person in the world we would ever think would receive His love. Praying for One moves you beyond prejudices, snap judgments, and assumptions that some people are beyond Christ's reach. God will push your comfort level and you will end up reaching people you never thought you would even speak to.

This story is from Joseph. Joseph prays for One and he serves breakfast every Saturday and Sunday in a local park to people in need. He meets all types of different people, but in this story God moved him even farther out of his comfort zone. Joseph writes:

The Lord doesn't let us pick who our One is. He tends to give us the One who puts us out of our comfort zone the most, but he always provides One.

One morning while serving breakfast to the homeless downtown, I prayed for Jesus to give me One with whom to share His love. Soon I began talking to a belligerent drunk I personally disliked. Jimmy was loud and obnoxious and routinely disrupted the message by heckling the speaker.

This morning, however, was a bit different. He was very morose, filled with self–loathing, and noticeably upset due to a fight he had with his girlfriend. While talking to him, I felt the Lord lead me to bring Jimmy to church with us after breakfast. I thought that this was just about the

129

dumbest idea ever. There was no way I was taking a visibly drunk and loud man to church.

A little later, I found myself again talking to Jimmy about his troubles and how the Lord loves and cares for him. Again, I felt the Lord tell me to bring him to church. Again, I said no way.

As we were packing up, I realized that this was the One the Lord picked for me, and I yielded to His request. I invited Jimmy to church while secretly hoping he would reject my offer.

Jimmy shocked me when he said yes. Once I got him to finish the beer tucked inside his vest, we set off for church.

We were coming up to a traffic light when he pulled another beer out of his vest and started drinking it. I gave him the choice to stay with his beer and walk back downtown or to stay with me and go to church. He chose to stay with me instead of the beer, so I took the beer, pulled over, and threw it in the trash.

Walking into the church building was when the fun really started. Jimmy insisted on greeting people by saying, "God bless...I'm the Devil." I was a bit embarrassed and very concerned about how to get Jimmy under control. I knew that I was in way over my head and that it was inevitable that Jimmy would cause a scene.

I was acting on faith alone that Jesus knew what He was doing and that I wasn't completely deranged to bring this man to church. As the service started, he became completely engrossed in the music. Then his attention was drawn to the pastor talking about, of all things, everyone having an addiction. It was then I realized that this was the message Jesus wanted him to hear. Afterward, we spent an hour-and-a-half talking about Jesus and His great love for us. It was then that I believe the Lord began to change Jimmy's heart.

Since then Jimmy married his girlfriend, and they now have an apartment. It is the first time in more than thirteen years that he is off of the streets. Others stepped up and provided furniture, dishes, cookware, and other necessities needed to make their apartment a home. He also received the first Christmas tree and decorations in what seemed to him like forever.

The Lord also used this opportunity to teach me a lesson about judging others and thinking there are those who are too far gone to bother trying to save. I had judged Jimmy and chalked him up as another panhandling drunk who was just looking to score a free meal and a buck for another beer. Looking at Jimmy through Jesus' eyes that morning, I stopped judging, listened to his troubles, and tried showing him the love and grace Jesus shows me daily. I still find myself way outside of my comfort zone, but it is reassuring to know I am doing the work He has commanded me to do.

Jimmy still has a difficult time understanding how Jesus and "church people" can love him, but he feels God's love and thanks Him for all the things that he is receiving. He is still working on sobriety and has made many big steps toward that goal.

I am truly blessed to witness His work on my One. Taking Jimmy to church wasn't the dumbest idea after all. No one is beyond God's reach!

God loves to teach us about His love while He uses us to share His love with others. Praying for One creates a new worldview where miracles are not only possible...they are expected. Saying "no" to God gets harder and harder, because you cannot bear the thought of missing out on a pray for One opportunity.

Praying for One sets the stage for simple steps of obedience. God is always speaking, directing, and working upstream in our lives. It is easy to miss out on what God is doing when you are not tuned into His will. When the number one desire of your heart is in line with Christ's mission to seek and save the lost, your steps will sync up with the Holy Spirit and all manner of weirdness will ensue.

You will become sensitive to God's voice. When He speaks, obedience will be your first response. "Yes Lord" will be on your lips. At His direction you will smile at people, offer a kind word, and extend a gentle touch. Random act of kindness will no longer be random. You will be consistently and intentionally kind. Every appointment will be divine, because everyone is a One.

The best weirdness of all is the fruit of the Holy Spirit.

"But the fruit of the Spirit is love, joy, peace, patience, kindness, goodness, faithfulness, gentleness and self-control. Against such things there is no law. Those who belong to Christ Jesus have crucified the sinful nature with its passions and desires. ̄Since we live by the Spirit let us keep in step with the Spirit."
Galatians 5:21-25

The normative pattern of this world is sin and selfishness. Pursuing Christ leads you into the depths of His divine nature. You will get in over your head and find yourself completely dependent on Jesus. In that beautiful place of total submission, you will become available to God. You will be a resource in His hands to accomplish His will.

People will get saved, because weird works.

A TALE OF TWO KINGDOMS

chapter ten

A TALE OF TWO KINGDOMS

Every day you are faced with a critical choice. Whose kingdom will you build?

Your life will be spent on one of two pursuits. You will either live to build your personal kingdom, or you will live to build Christ's eternal Kingdom.

If you long to build Christ's Kingdom, you must make this choice each and every day. The universal reality of sin and the fallen nature of humanity set our default choice to personal kingdom building. The prevailing attitudes of our culture all center on selfishness, greed, and self-glorification. Failing to build Christ's Kingdom intentionally will lead automatically to the secondary pursuit of looking out for #1.

Our world constantly projects the self-serving message, "Look out for #1."

If we do not actively submit to Jesus and His mission, we easily slip back into the nature of sin and selfishness. The beauty of praying for One is that it causes us to actively choose to participate in building Christ's Kingdom.

The phrase "Look out for #1" takes on a whole new meaning for followers of Jesus. We are blissfully aware that each One is one more person Jesus died for. Each One is one more for the Kingdom of Heaven. We are always on the lookout for #1, but the focus is decidedly off of self and is fixed on finding One more for Jesus.

When you pray for One, you make the conscious choice to build Christ's Kingdom. If you fail to make this choice, your life will go into default mode, and you will build a worthless, temporary kingdom for self. It is important to take an inventory of your life regularly. Ask the Lord to search your heart and reveal what you are living for. Dig deep and examine your baseline motivations.

What drives you? What compels you to action? What excites you? What stories do you long to tell? What is your predominant prayer?

One of the best diagnostic questions to ask is, "Am I available to the Lord?"

There is a strong temptation to compartmentalize our lives. We set aside specific times that we are available to serve Jesus. If Jesus calls us to action during what we have deemed to be "His" time, then we jump at the opportunity and faithfully serve. But if He calls during a predetermined break, then He's going to have to wait. The problem is that Jesus does not wait, and if we refuse to do His work, the task will go undone.

Constant availability is a foundational principle for following Christ. When He says, "Go," we go. When He says, "Speak," we speak. When He says, "Jump," we do not waste time on silly questions like "How high?" We just jump and depend on Jesus to do the rest.

I pray for One every day, but that doesn't mean that I am always available to the Lord. I often find myself compartmentalizing my life into time that I am available to God and times that I am not. It is kind of like putting a "do not disturb" sign on a hotel room door. If I am not exceptionally careful, I will sequester myself from God. I shut Him out at certain times and make myself off-limits to Him.

God is not cool with my unavailability. In fact, He often answers my prayers for One when I am huddled in my private space with the deadbolt turned, the chain securely fastened, and the "do not disturb" sign in place. When I retreat into my personal world, the Lord stands at the door and knocks. It turns out that Jesus is not a fan of restricted areas. When He becomes your Lord, Jesus is given an all-access pass to every element of your life. Close a door on Him, and He will knock. And knock. And knock.

We must choose to maintain an open-door policy. It will not happen by accident. Again, the default mode is to hide away and build a private kingdom based on self. We must make conscious decisions to build Christ's Kingdom instead of our own. Praying for One works as a doorstop to keep your life open to the work of seeking and saving the lost. Praying for One puts you at the ready for when Jesus calls. The risk of compartmentalization is reduced tremendously because there is no such thing as "me-time." There is only "Jesus-time."

I enjoy working out. I go to the gym each weekday morning. It is part of my regular rhythm and routine. I look forward to my time at the gym because I put my headphones on and zone out from the rest of the world for a while. My workouts are an important part of my relationship with God, but if I am not careful, I can miss opportunities to share His love with others.

Personally, I blame the mirrors.

There are just too many mirrors at the gym. Everywhere I look, there are mirrors, and in each mirror, I see me. So often, when I am working out, my perspective changes. Instead of looking at everyone through the lens of praying for One and with a godly perspective, I see them only through the lens of self. Of course, that is if I see them at all. Sometimes I am so fixated on the image in those blasted mirrors that I see nothing but me.

When I am not careful, the gym becomes the dreaded "me-time." I wonder how many Ones I have missed sharing the love of Jesus with because I was unavailable. When I slip into the default mode of personal kingdom-building, I find myself completely unaware of what I am missing out on.

I recently found myself engaged in the battle to determine which kingdom to build while at the gym. I was pretty excited because all through my workout I prayed for One. I smiled at people. I said, "Hi." I was on alert for any opening to share the love of Jesus. I looked at every person like they could be the One.

One of the neat benefits of praying for One is that God will remove prejudices from your heart. Over the years, Jesus has worked to deliver me from all kinds of prejudicial thinking. Since anyone could be the One, God has revealed how crucial it is to put aside preconceived judgments and discriminatory fears. Things like race, age, social status, and economic position can become roadblocks to sharing Christ with others.

I would love to declare that I am prejudice-free, but there are still certain people who I refuse to share the love of Jesus with. And of course, one of them walked into the gym that day.

I had just finished my workout and was grabbing one last drink at the water fountain when I looked up and saw him. Okay, I did not actually see him. What I saw was his hideous t-shirt. It was this disgusting burnt orange color with a white longhorn across the chest. He was wearing a University of Texas shirt.

Most people could probably get over this man's poor choice of clothing, but I am a graduate of Texas A&M University, and Aggies do not like Longhorns. It just isn't natural. The two universities are rivals, and as a graduate of A&M, I will admit that we Aggies may have a bit of inferiority complex. Over the years, the Longhorns have flooded the great state of Texas with their burnt orange paraphernalia. For some bizarre reason, the masses have been duped into thinking that they look good in that ridiculous color.

One of the benefits of living in New Hampshire is that I am over 2,000 miles away from the University of Texas. When you live in Texas, your eyes kind of adjust to the constant barrage of burnt orange you are forced to behold on a daily basis. The standard joke is that, if you see someone wearing a Texas A&M shirt, you know that the person probably went to school at A&M, but if you see someone wearing a Longhorns shirt, the person probably went to Wal-Mart. Having lived in New Hampshire for a couple of years caused me to forget about my prejudices toward Longhorn fans because I rarely encounter them this far north.

So when I looked up and saw that t-shirt, I was in a little bit of shock. It was so utterly out of place, and I was perplexed as to why someone in New Hampshire would wear it. Did this man lose a bet? Was he vision-impaired and being victimized by a cruel caretaker? Had he received this shirt as a gag gift and felt obligated

141

to wear it in public? Could he possibly be from Texas and actually like the Longhorns?

As I pondered the possibilities, I felt a familiar urge. It was the Holy Spirit-driven, pray for One urge. I was supposed to share God's love with the guy in the Longhorns shirt. I had never seen this man before, but the shirt provided an easy way to begin a conversation. All I needed to do was ask him why a guy in New Hampshire was wearing a shirt from Texas.

I easily envisioned the entire conversation. I would tell him that I was from Texas and then make a little joke about the Longhorns. He would chuckle and ask what brought me to New Hampshire. I would respond by telling him that I am a pastor of church in the area. He would ask which one. I would tell him how amazing our church is and then invite him. He would say that he would love to come because he has never been to a church before. I would find out his name and from then on greet him by name and remind him about the invitation to come to church. I would pray for him everyday and begin to have meaningful conversations whenever I saw him at the gym. I would find out about his family, his job, his struggles, and so on. We would become friends, and I would introduce him to Jesus.

I could see the whole scenario, but in that moment, I froze. When I looked up from the water fountain no words came out of my mouth. The man just walked by me and into the locker room. I stood there for a few seconds and realized that I had missed a pray for One opportunity. I felt pretty crummy about not responding to God's leading, so I started to rationalize the whole thing away. I thought about how weird it would have been to start a conversation with someone about how much I hated his wardrobe choice. I convinced myself that he was not really my One for that day and that God would provide someone else.

With that frame of mind, I went into the locker room to shower. During my shower, I prayed. As I prayed, God made it clear that I had been disobedient. I told God I was sorry for not talking to the guy. I asked God to give me another chance. I prayed for One.

When I came out of the shower and rounded the corner toward my locker, guess who I ran into? That's right...Longhorn t-shirt guy. I actually bumped into him, but the only words that came out my mouth were "excuse me." He muttered something back and continued on his way. Again I felt the Holy Spirit urge me to speak to this guy, but I did not do it. I watched him walk away for the second time, and I knew that I had blown it again.

I started to chase him down, but all I had on was a towel. I completely psyched myself out as I thought about trying to share the love of Jesus with a complete stranger while I was half naked. I hung my head in disappointment and went to my locker to get dressed. I continued to pray while I put my clothes on. I told God that I was sorry and that I would get the next One. I promised God that I would be bolder and more obedient.

As I walked out of the locker room to head to my car, I was reading an email on my phone. My eyes were down, and if Longhorn t-shirt guy had not physically bumped into me, I would not have seen him at all. I looked up from my phone and was shocked to have a third opportunity to start a conversation with the guy. This time, he said, "Excuse me," and I muttered something back. He gave me this strange look of recognition like he was waiting to have a conversation since it was the third time we had run into each other in a thirty-minute period.

When I looked back down at my phone, he kind of shrugged his shoulders and walked away. I took three steps forward and froze. I stood still and prayed. I could not believe that I had blown three pray for One opportunities with the same guy in less than thirty minutes. I am not sure how long I stood there contemplating my next move.

Finally, I decided to go back into the locker room to talk to him. There was just one problem...I had no idea what he looked like. I had not actually looked at his face. I did not know his height, hair color, or even ethnicity. All I had seen was that burnt orange t-shirt.

When I went back into the locker room, there was not a burnt orange t-shirt in sight. He had changed clothes, and I had no way of identifying him. I received some pretty awkward stares as I walked through the locker room looking everybody over. I looked, but I could not find the guy.

I failed. Seriously...I failed. There is no happy ending to this story. I did not find the guy the next day or the day after that. I did not see that same t-shirt a month later. There was never a conversation, an invitation to church, or a gospel presentation. I had a chance, and I missed it.

I failed because I allowed a prejudice to slip me back into the default mode of personal kingdom-building. I talk to people all the time who, for some reason, cannot handle the notion of failure. They like to say things like, "Failure is not an option."

Failure is always an option.

Praying for One does not guarantee success. God will answer the prayer. He will make you aware of opportunities. God will place an intense love for the lost deep in your heart, put people who do not know Him yet directly in your path, and nudge you to share His love with them. But you must make a choice. Which kingdom will you build?

144

I find this to be the most troubling part of God's plan. I do not want failure to be an option, but He chose me to be His ambassador, and I am painfully aware of my many shortcomings. On one hand it is an honor to know the Master's business and to have meaningful purpose, but on the other hand I am disturbed by the reality of the mission. If I do not do what God has called me to do, then it does not get done.

The gravity of this truth is essential to grasp. Failure is always an option. If we refuse to recognize this reality, we end up living in a land of make believe. We will explain away failure and make up little scenarios in hopes of finding comfort.

In the case of Longhorn t-shirt guy, I could easily placate myself by thinking, "God will send someone else," or "God was just trying to teach me a lesson." I can pretend that I did not fail because God got my attention and I learned something.

But I did fail. I prayed for One. God provided One. I failed to act.

Praying for One is about more people in the Kingdom of Heaven. We will never accidently fall into building Christ's Kingdom. We must intentionally choose to do it.

Recognizing and owning failure is important, because it causes us to deal with the grief, guilt, shame, and remorse that accompanies sin. When we pretend that we do not fail or that it does not matter if we fail, then sin is readily accepted and the default choice of personal kingdom building is made. Knowing that failure is always an option keeps us at the ready and primes us to choose to build Christ's Kingdom.

Your life is a tale of two kingdoms. In the end, only one kingdom will remain. Make the choice to build the Kingdom of Heaven.

I TRIPLE DOG DARE YOU

chapter eleven

I TRIPLE DOG DARE YOU

I love Easter.

I'm not putting it on par with Christmas, but I do love it.

Christmas is my number one holiday for obvious reasons... presents. On the holiday celebration scale, Easter is below Christmas for the simple fact that the gift giving and receiving aspect is far less substantial. In that regard, Easter cannot really compete with Christmas.

However, if you took Christmas out of the equation, then Easter would be my favorite.

Easter is a special time of celebration for many reasons. The resurrection of Jesus is the single greatest thing to ever happen on planet earth. Easter commemorates that event as families gather together, go to church, and enjoy a delicious, home-cooked meal. Easter marks the end of winter and the beginning of spring. It reminds us of new life and how all that was dead can be revived.

Everything about Easter is great, but my favorite part is the Easter baskets. Easter mornings brought great excitement as I woke up early to search for my basket. I have amazing memories of digging through fake grass to find every last morsel of candy.

Inside plastic eggs, there were jellybeans, gumdrops, marshmallow chicks, egg-shaped chocolates with crunchy malted centers, and foil-wrapped chocolate eggs with sweetly delicious insides that looked like yolks. The plastic eggs formed a perimeter of sorts surrounding the centerpiece of the basket. It was as if the eggs were bowing down before the piece de resistance of all Easter candy...the Chocolate Easter Bunny.

I mean the solid chocolate Easter Bunny, not the cheap hollow version. A solid chocolate Easter Bunny can last a kid for weeks if it is eaten correctly. A well-placed nibble here and there has actually been known to stretch Easter all the way into May for some disciplined children. Employ the right strategy on solid chocolate Easter bunny eating, and you have a gift that keeps on giving.

On one particular Easter morning, I woke up and went in search of my Easter basket. I was at a transitional age where my Mom and Dad wanted to move me from the frivolity of youth into a deeper understanding of the meaning of Easter. While I appreciate their intent, their methodology left much to be desired.

I found my Easter basket, but there were no delicious candy treats nestled inside. The fake grass concealed nothing of value.

The only candy I found was an old and cracked white jellybean that had gotten lodged in the wicker on the bottom of the basket left over from some Easter past. It tasted like a stale, semisweet, chewy communion cracker.

Instead of candy, my Easter basket contained an assortment of flower seeds and gardening tools. These are not the things that adolescent boys dream of. I made my disappointment clear. Easter was ruined.

I spent the remainder of the day pouting. My Mom and older sister went outside in the afternoon to plant a flower garden. They invited me to join them, but I refused. They took my sister's seeds and carefully planted them in the backyard, but I just threw my seeds on a shelf in my room. In the weeks that followed, every time I saw those seeds in my room, I got angry. I did not want seeds. I wanted candy. Those seeds sat on a shelf collecting dust and causing me angst.

One afternoon, my Mom and sister came through the house looking for the camera. They were both clearly excited about something in the backyard. I went outside with them to see what all the commotion was about. The flowers had bloomed. I took a few photos of them in front of their beautiful flower garden and I realized that I had totally missed out on something good.

I did not have a garden. All I had were seeds on a shelf.

Sadly, this is the experience that many who claim to follow Christ will have when they come to the end of their lives. They will look back at their years hoping to see a flower garden, but there will be only seeds on a shelf.

Seeds are only good if they are sown. Jesus calls us to participate in His mission of seeking and saving the lost, but for many, the transition from merely receiving grace to giving grace never occurs. One of the best things about following Jesus is that we are not just recipients of His Kingdom; we are participants in building His Kingdom. Jesus entrusts His mission to us and goes with us to plant, cultivate, and harvest.

Christ's words are clear in this regard:

"Then Jesus came to them and said, 'All authority in heaven and on earth has been given to me. Therefore go and make disciples of all nations, baptizing them in the name of the Father and of the Son and of the Holy Spirit, and teaching them to obey everything I have commanded you. And surely I am with you always, to the very end of the age.'"
Matthew 28:18-20

There is a point very early in your relationship with Jesus when it is crucial to move beyond every "what will I get out of this" kind of thinking. The focus must move from the frivolity of self to the seriousness of Christ's mission. We receive the gift of salvation and then we receive the gift of seeds.

God's desire is that none would perish.

"The Lord is not slow in keeping his promise, as some understand slowness. He is patient with you, not wanting anyone to perish, but everyone to come to repentance."
2 Peter 3:9

God's will cannot be done if we keep our seeds on a shelf. Life is a meaningless void of nothingness apart from the mission of Jesus. We have the amazing opportunity to celebrate Easter every day. When we plant seeds by sharing Christ with others, we get to be eyewitnesses to the resurrection of Christ within new believers!

Praying for One sets the stage for a huge harvest. Every day is about planting seeds. Each conversation cultivates the soil.

Seeds are taken off the shelf and scattered liberally. God's grace is limitless, so we never run out of seeds. There is never a need to be stingy with the gospel. When you follow Jesus, you want what He wants, and He wants a huge harvest.

"Remember this: Whoever sows sparingly will also reap sparingly, and whoever sows generously will also reap generously. Each man should give what he has decided in his heart to give, not reluctantly or under compulsion, for God loves a cheerful giver. And God is able to make all grace abound to you, so that in all things at all times, having all that you need, you will abound in every good work. As it is written:

'He has scattered abroad his gifts to the poor; his righteousness endures forever.'

Now he who supplies seed to the sower and bread for food will also supply and increase your store of seed and will enlarge the harvest of your righteousness. You will be made rich in every way so that you can be generous on every occasion, and through us your generosity will result in thanksgiving to God."

2 Corinthians 9:6-11

What will the end result of your life be? If it does not result in thanksgiving to God, then it will be wasted. The simple fact that you are still breathing means that you are here for a purpose. God wants to use you so that there will be more people in the Kingdom of Heaven.

Can it really be this simple? Can praying for One actually work in your life?

You will never know if you do not try it.

Many people have decided that evangelism is not for them. Some believe that this type of activity is just for the religiously trained.

153

Others are paralyzed by the fear of rejection. There are those who "tried it once" and had some form of a negative experience. Some worry about how others will perceive them. They do not want to be viewed as pushy, hyper-religious, judgmental, or Jesus-freaky.

Praying for One destroys the excuses because, when you pray for One, God changes your heart. His love drives out fear. His mercy removes prejudices. His mission replaces concern for self.

So, why not pray for One? What do you have to lose?

Do not let a bad evangelism experience or the lack of evangelistic experience keep you from sharing in the greatest mission the world has ever known. You will never know how great it is until you try it.

Isn't it strange how one negative experience can adversely impact a lifetime?

I had a run in with a can of spinach at a critical point in my life. I was in that golden age when cartoons still captivated and kissing was gross. I spent a week with my grandparents during the summer and made some amazing memories.

Most of those memories had to do with food. I belong to a family that loves to eat.

I remember that each afternoon at 3:00 p.m. my grandmother would lay a blanket out in front of the television. She would then serve me a snack on that blanket while I watched cartoons. Every day she brought me something different like peanut butter crackers, Cheetos, Nilla Wafers, Little Debbie snack cakes, or saltines with Easy Cheese. There was always a frosty mug of root beer to wash it down.

For breakfast we had donuts and coffee. I was far too young

for coffee, but when I watched my grandfather dunk his donut, I had to try it to. That got me started on a lifelong coffee obsession.

Dinner was a special time as the three of us gathered around their small kitchen table for a hot meal. There was always some sort of meat, a starch, a vegetable, and dessert. Of course dessert could only be eaten if you cleaned your plate.

Cleaning my plate was never much of a problem. I loved my grandmother's cooking, and dessert was sufficient motivation. One night, though, I just could not do it.

I blame Popeye for the situation that unfolded. Earlier that day, as I watched cartoons, I declared to my grandparents that I wanted to be just like Popeye. Popeye was an ordinary guy, but when he ate spinach, he became super strong. He carried a can of spinach in his pocket for emergency situations. Whenever his archenemy, Brutus, got the upper hand, all Popeye had to do was open up a can.

I begged my grandmother to fix me some spinach. That turned out to be a huge mistake.

She found a can of spinach that she had stashed in the back of the pantry. I was not prepared for the dark green, slimy, foul-smelling glob of disgustingness that came out of that can. She heated it up on the stove and served it with dinner.

When she scooped it onto my plate, I instantly realized that there would be no dessert for me. There was no way that stuff was going to go into my mouth. I no longer wanted to be like Popeye. The cost was just too high.

After a great deal of coercion, guilt, and a few threats, they convinced me to try one bite. It was awful. It tasted worse than it looked and smelled. I was wounded for life.

155

I made a decision that day that I did not like spinach. In fact, I decided that I did not like green vegetables of any kind. For years I refused to eat them. I was outspoken against them. I ridiculed vegetable eaters and would not listen to reason.

Finally someone put my manhood to the test by daring me to eat some spinach. They told me that it was fresh spinach and that it was different from the slimy canned stuff I had tried as a kid. I put a small piece in my mouth and found that I did not gag. I tried another piece and discovered that I did indeed like it.

It turns out that I enjoy all kinds of green vegetables. I love broccoli, brussels sprouts, peas, green beans, and asparagus (even though it makes my pee smell funny). I can't believe that I missed out on something so wonderful for so long just because I wouldn't try it.

Now what about you?

Will you pray for One? Will you try it?

I dare you. I triple dog dare you.

FROM BILL

chapter twelve

FROM BILL

I have received hundreds of Praying for One stories. All of them are impactful, powerful, and inspiring. I would love to include them all in this book, but time and space do not allow for such indulgences.

I have returned to one story over and over again throughout the writing of this book. The story is simple, short, and thoroughly profound. This story captures the essence of praying for One, and I leave it for you to ponder in your heart.

The following was taken from an email that was sent to me by a man named Bill.

A neighbor found her down by the river, no shoes or socks, her feet dirty and bleeding.

She was crying and hysterical.

He brought her to us, because he knew we would help her.

We hugged her and told her we loved her. We knelt down, took a warm washcloth from the kitchen, and washed her feet. We found a pair of socks and shoes her size and put them on her feet. We fed, hugged, and prayed with her.

She accepted Christ that morning, and we were joyous.

Three days later she died of a drug overdose, and we were devastated.

We were consoled that God knew she would die that week. He wanted her to accept His son before she died, so He brought her to us.

We prayed for One, God sent One to us, and now she is with Him for eternity.

We continue to pray for One.

- Bill

Then Jesus told them this parable: "Suppose one of you has a hundred sheep and loses one of them. Doesn't he leave the ninety-nine in the open country and go after the lost sheep until he finds it? And when he finds it, he joyfully puts it on his shoulders and goes home. Then he calls his friends and neighbors together and says, 'Rejoice with me; I have found my lost sheep.' I tell you that in the same way there will be more rejoicing in heaven over one sinner who repents than over ninety-nine righteous persons who do not need to repent.

Luke 15:3-7

About the Author

Bo Chancey is the Senior Pastor of Manchester Christian Church in Manchester, New Hampshire. He is a gifted communicator who is passionate about challenging people to fall madly in love with Jesus Christ and believes that God desperately desires all people to find the freedom of living an abundant life in Him.

Bo received a degree in History and Speech Communications at Texas A&M University. He and his wife, Somer, have three children: Alizah, Aysen and Ensley. Bo enjoys sports, working creatively, spending time with his family and preaching.

facebook.com/bochancey

twitter.com/bochancey

For more information, visit bochancey.com.

Other Books by Bo

I'm Going to Light Myself on Fire

Every Day with Jesus

What's Your Problem

Another Day with Jesus

Don't Say "$#%&X" in Church!

Find these and other titles at amazon.com.

visit **prayforone.com** to find:

- A 41 Day Prayer & Devotion Guide to go along with your reading of *Pray for One*.

- Materials for groups, including videos and a leader's guide.

- Other great resources for you and your church.